AQA English and English Language

Foundation Tier

GCSE

New College
New College Drive
Swindon SN3 1AH
Tel: 01793 611470

Jo Mulliner

Imelda Pilgrim

Malcolm Seccombe

Julia Waines

Malcolm J. White

Series Editor

Imelda Pilgrim

Nelson Thornes

Text © Jo Mulliner, Imelda Pilgrim, Malcolm Seccombe, Julia Waines, Malcolm J. White
Original illustrations © Nelson Thornes Ltd 2010

The right of Jo Mulliner, Imelda Pilgrim, Malcolm Seccombe, Julia Waines and Malcolm J. White to be identified as authors of this work has been asserted by them in accordance with the Copyright, Designs and Patents Act 1988.

All rights reserved. No part of this publication may be reproduced or transmitted in any form or by any means, electronic or mechanical, including photocopy, recording or any information storage and retrieval system, without permission in writing from the publisher or under licence from the Copyright Licensing Agency Limited, of Saffron House, 6–10 Kirby Street, London, EC1N 8TS.

Any person who commits any unauthorised act in relation to this publication may be liable to criminal prosecution and civil claims for damages.

Published in 2010 by:
Nelson Thornes Ltd
Delta Place
27 Bath Road
CHELTENHAM
GL53 7TH
United Kingdom

10 11 12 13 14 / 10 9 8 7 6 5 4 3 2 1

A catalogue record for this book is available from the British Library

ISBN 978 1 4085 0596 0

Cover photograph: Heather Gunn Photography
Page make-up by Pantek Arts Ltd
Illustrations by Mark Draisey and Angela Knowles with additional illustrations by Pantek Arts Ltd
Printed and bound in Spain by GraphyCems

Acknowledgements

The authors and publisher would like to thank the following for permission to reproduce material.

Source texts: p8 © Crown Copyright; p17 Blood Brothers by Willy Russell, Methuen Drama, an imprint of A&C Black Publishers; p25 Ronald Grant Archive; p31 Advertising Archives; p32 Suzuki GB PLC; p33 'Island Man' from The Fat Black Woman's Poems by Grace Nichols, Virago, a division of Little Brown Book Group; p45 David Rowan; p54 Manchester Evening News; p59 ©1994 Tatamkhulu Afrika, from: Maqabane, Mayibuye, South Africa; p66 Liz Loxley; p72 Reproduced by permission of the Royal National Lifeboat Institution; p73 best-family-beach-vacations.com; Go Ape!; p74 from The Boys are back in Town by Simon Carr, published by Arrow. Reprinted by permission of The Random House Group Ltd; p119 Coalition to Stop the Use of Child Soldiers www.child-soldiers.org; p123 © The Sun 5 June 2009/nisyndication.com; p127 Blood Brothers by Willy Russell, Methuen Drama, an imprint of A&C Black Publishers; p129 Clare Wigfall, When the Wasp Drowned taken from The Loudest Sound and Nothing, 2007, Faber and Faber Ltd; p130 Copyright © Jackie Kay 1992; p133 © Harewood House Trust. Harewood House is an Educational Charitable Trust and welcomes educational visits. www.harewood.org; p135 Reader's Digest Association Limited; p136 Go Ape!; p139 In the Middle of the Night, Robert Cormier, 1998. Reproduced by permission of Penguin Books Ltd; p141 'Daz 4 Zoe', Robert Swindells 1990. Reproduced by permission of Penguin Books Ltd; from The Grey King by Susan Cooper, published by The Bodley Head. Reprinted by permission of The Random House Group Ltd; p142 An Inspector Calls and Other Plays, J.B.Priestley. First published by William Heineman 1948-50, first published by Penguin Book 1969, Penguin Classics 2000. 'An Inspector Calls' copyright 1947 by J.B.Priestley. Reproduced by the permission of Penguin Books Ltd; p192 Article reprinted with the permission of eHow, Inc., www.ehow.com; **Photographs:** p1(a) Alamy/Golden Pixels LLC, (b) Alamy/ Dave Porter, (c) Rex Features/Sipa Press; p2 Alamy/ Photo Network; p4 (a) Alamy/ Barry Morgan (b) Getty/ Fred Duval/FilmMagic; p5 Fotolia; p6 Fotolia; p8 Getty/Gary Ombler; p23 Fotolia; p25 Ronald Grant Archive; p31 Advertising Archives; p32 Suzuki; p33 Photolibrary/ Randa Bishop; p34 Getty/Michael McQueen; p42 Fotolia; p45 Alamy/Peter Dench; p47 (a) Alamy/Keith Morris, (b) Alamy/Ace Stock Limited; p50 (a) Fotolia (b) Getty/Gallo Images (c) Fotolia; p54 Alamy/travelib Europe; p56 Alamy/Robert Harding Picture Library Ltd; p58 Link/Eric Miller; p60 (a & b) Sorrentotourism. com; p62 Fotolia; p64 (a) Getty/Sean Gallup, (b)Getty/ Bloomberg; p66 Getty/Photodisc; p81 Getty/Image Source; p83 Fotolia; p87 Rex Features/Eye Candy,; p93 Transworld; p106 Alamy/Directphoto.org; p108 Fotolia x2; p111 Rex Features/ Everett Collection; p119 Alamy/Mike Goldwater; p120 (a) Random House/Vintage (b) Little, Brown/Atom; p122 Jeffrey Evans; p123 Getty/Visuals Unlimited; p126 Alamy/Caro; p132 (a) DK Images, (b) Alamy/Ken Welsh,(c) Alamy/Atlanpic; p137 Xscape; p138 Getty/Samir Hussein; p139 Alamy/Victor Watts; p142 Julia Waines; p145 Education Photos/ John Walmsley; p150 Education Photos/ John Walmsley; p152 Penguin; p158 (a) Photolibrary/Creatas, (b) Photolibrary; p169 Ronald Grant Archive; p188 Jenny Gunn Photography; p189 (a) Fotolia, (b) Fotolia, (c) Fotolia, (d) iStockphoto; p190 Rex Features/ ITV; p195 (a) Alamy/Oote Boe Photography 2, (b) Photolibrary/Boutet Jean-Pierre; p197 Getty/Hulton Archive.

Every effort has been made to contact the copyright holders and we apologise if any have been overlooked. Should copyright have been unwittingly infringed in this book, the owners should contact the publishers, who will make the corrections at reprint.

Contents

AQA GCSE English and GCSE English Language

Nelson Thornes and AQA

Nelson Thornes has worked in partnership with AQA to ensure that the student book and the accompanying online resources offer you the best support possible for your GCSE course. The print and online resources together **unlock blended learning**; this means that the links between the activities in the book and the activities online blend together to maximise your understanding of a topic and help you to achieve your potential.

All AQA-endorsed resources undergo a thorough quality assurance process to ensure that their contents closely match the AQA specification. You can be confident that the content of materials branded with AQA's 'Exclusively Endorsed' logo have been written, checked and approved by AQA senior examiners, in order to achieve AQA's exclusive endorsement.

About your course

This book has been written to guide you through your GCSE English or GCSE English Language. It will help you to develop skills you need to succeed, not only in your exams and assessments, but in whatever you decide to do afterwards.

You will either be studying for a GCSE in English or English Language. If you are studying GCSE English, you will be doing literature as part of this course. If you are studying GCSE English Language, you will also be taking GCSE English Literature.

Parts of this book are designed to develop your skills in reading, writing and communicating about a range of texts: non-fiction, literature, media and transcripts. So, whichever route through your GCSE you take, you will be well prepared.

How to use this book

The first three sections of the book each cover a key English skill:

- Reading
- Writing
- Speaking and listening

You will be assessed on each of these skills either by an exam or through a controlled assessment. After you've worked through each section, you are shown how to use these skills effectively when being assessed in the 'Making your skills count' chapters.

The fourth section of the book covers spoken language, which is tested only in GCSE English Language.

The final section of the book covers the basic rules of punctuation and spelling. Remember, you will gain marks for being able to spell and punctuate your work accurately.

The features in this book include:

Objectives

At the beginning of each chapter you will find a list of learning objectives that contain targets linked to the requirements of the specification.

Activity

Activities to develop and reinforce the skills focus for the lesson.

Check your learning

A list of points at the end of the chapter that summarise what you have covered.

Some (but not all) chapters feature:

Biography · Background

Biographies and backgrounds provide you with additional information about a writer or a text.

Key terms

Key term: term that you will find it useful to be able to define and understand. The definitions also appear in the glossary at the end of the student book.

Make a note

Useful points for you to keep a note of.

Review and reflect

Opportunities for peer and/or self-assessment.

Speaking and listening

Specific activities testing speaking and listening skills.

Stretch yourself

Extension activities to take the work in a chapter further.

Top tip

Guidance from the examiners or moderators on how to avoid common pitfalls and mistakes, and how to achieve the best marks in the exam or controlled assessment.

Online resources

These online resources are available on **kerboodle!** which can be accessed via the internet at **www.kerboodle.com/live**, anytime, anywhere.

If your school or college subscribes to **kerboodle!** you will be provided with your own personal login details. Once logged in, access your course and locate the required activity.

Throughout the book you will see this icon **k!** whenever there is a relevant interactive activity available in **kerboodle!**.

Please visit **kerboodle.helpserve.com** if you would like more information and help on how to use **kerboodle!**.

Weblinks for this book

Because Nelson Thornes is not responsible for third party content online, there may be some changes to this material that are beyond our control. In order for us to ensure that the links referred to are as up-to-date and stable as possible, please let us know at webadmin@nelsonthornes.com if you find a link that doesn't work and we will do our best to redirect these, or to list an alternative site.

Reading plays a part in almost every area of our lives. We read to:

- learn new things
- find out about the world we live in
- work out how to make things
- access essential information
- catch up on our friends and family
- experience pleasure and enjoyment.

Aims of the Reading section

The qualification you are studying will equip you to use your reading skills in a range of situations, including:

- school and college courses after GCSEs
- work-based learning
- personal and business communications
- reading for pleasure.

You will be able to revise the skills you already have, and extend and develop them. You will learn how to find information quickly, understand the main ideas in a text you read and work out how professional writers use language for particular effects.

Don't worry, you will not be expected to do all of this straight away. The activities will help you to gradually improve your skills and work on each aspect so you have the chance to build up your confidence.

Activities

The activities in Reading will allow you to work in pairs or small groups on many occasions so that you learn and build confidence together. You will read a variety of texts, stories and information texts in many forms including posters, leaflets, advertisements, etc. Written tasks will show you how to prepare for the Reading paper in the exam at GCSE and for controlled assessments. You will have the opportunity to see sample answers and to develop the way you write about the reading you have done.

Assessments

The chapters each address differing aspects of the GCSE course. At the start of each chapter, you will know what area you are going to be working on and what you should be able to achieve by the time you have finished the different tasks.

There are two forms of assessment:

- controlled assessment
- exam.

The Reading section will help you to prepare for both of these types of assessment.

1

Objectives

In this chapter you will:

learn how to text mark a text

develop your skills in skimming and scanning

use presentational clues to help you find information.

Finding information

We read all sorts of things for all sorts of reasons. We read on-screen and on paper. One important reason for reading is to find information. In this chapter, you will learn how to find information you need quickly and efficiently.

Text marking

Sometimes when we read, we need to remember particular details. Text marking, or making notes on a text, helps you to record things you notice when you read a passage. This is also called annotating a text. You can underline or highlight particular words, phrases or sentences and write notes in the margin.

Look at Text A. The student was asked to read the text and answer the question: 'Give five reasons why judo is such a popular sport.' The student has marked the five reasons using highlighting and made notes in the margin.

Judo

Judo is a very popular sport. To begin with, it is a sport for both males and females. Many clubs have thriving senior and junior sections with children as young as five learning how to throw and how to fall safely. It is also a sport for all shapes and sizes. To take part in judo you do not have to have a particular shape or size. Judo is practised by people of all proportions. A club will usually pair up players of roughly the same size and weight. Within weeks, players often say how much they have gained in confidence. They are fitter, know how to fall safely and how to throw an opponent. For those who are competitive, judo offers opportunities to train hard, gain belts for their expertise, compete against others, from club right up to Olympic standard. For others, however, judo is a place to make friends and have fun. Why not try it?

For both sexes

Anyone can take part

Builds confidence

People can progress

You can socialise and make friends

2

Activity

1

a Text B is about why and how cars are shaped in a particular way. You need to answer the question: 'How does the shape of a car help its driver?'

Either: Choose and write down three things that answer the question and put these into your own words.

Or: If you have a copy of the text, highlight and annotate it as shown in Text A above.

b Share your ideas with a partner and discuss any differences you have. Adjust your notes if you need to.

Car design

For many years, cars have been designed with particular attention paid to their shape. Car makers have come up with a variety of ideas that make cutting through that 'wall' of air easier. Basically, having a car designed with airflow in mind means it has less difficulty picking up speed. It can achieve more miles per litre because the engine doesn't have to work as hard to push the car through the wall of air. Engineers have developed several ways of doing this. More rounded designs and shapes on the outside of the vehicle help to channel air so that it flows around the car easily. Some high-performance cars even have parts that move air smoothly across the underside of the car. Many also include a spoiler – also known as a rear wing – to stop the air from lifting the car's wheels and making it unstable at high speeds.

Skimming and scanning

Skimming

Skimming a text involves reading very quickly to get a general sense of what the text is about. One good way to do this is to read the first sentence in each paragraph. Writers often tell us what a paragraph is going to be about in their first sentence. This is sometimes called the **topic sentence**. Look at Text C taken from a magazine article about Newcastle.

Key terms

Skimming: reading a text quickly to get an idea of what it is about.

Topic sentence: a sentence often used at the start of a paragraph that shows what the paragraph will be about.

Ⓒ Newcastle

First sentence refers to interesting places

The city is full of interesting landmarks. The Keep is the castle on the banks of the River Tyne that gave the city its name. It towers over the historic quayside from which great ships once ferried coal around the world. Standing proudly on the quay is Bessie Surtees house, a genuine Tudor building in a fine state of repair. A short climb will

Rest of paragraph provides detail of places

take you to Grey Street, one of Europe's finest examples of Edwardian architecture. Perhaps, however, the city is proudest of a more recent building, St. James' Park, home of Newcastle United, and one of the finest football stadia in Europe.

Activity

2 As quickly as you can, skim to read the following two paragraphs about Comic Relief in Text D and answer the questions that follow.

Ⓓ

1 Red Nose Day is a UK-wide fundraising event organised by Comic Relief every two years. On Red Nose Day everyone is encouraged to put on a Red Nose and do something a little bit silly to raise money – celebrities included! People of all ages across the whole of the UK hold sponsored events, wear funny costumes, bake cakes and sell all kinds of things to raise money.

2 It ends in a night of extraordinary comedy and moving documentary films on BBC1. It's an event that unites the entire nation in trying to make a difference to the lives of thousands of people, both across Africa and in the UK, who face terrible injustice or who live in dreadful poverty. Well-known comedians give their time freely and phone lines across the country are manned by volunteers.

a Which of the following answers best describes the purpose of paragraph 1?

   i It tells the reader about the work done by the Comic Relief charity.

   ii It gives a brief description of what takes place on the evening of Red Nose Day.

   iii It encourages the reader to donate to Comic Relief.

b Which of the following answers best describes the purpose of paragraph 2?

   i It gives examples of the fundraising activities in past years.

   ii It gives a brief description of what takes place on the evening of Red Nose Day.

   iii It encourages the reader to donate to Comic Relief.

Skimming is a skill that improves with practice. The more you practise, the quicker you will be at working out what a text is about.

Scanning

Sometimes we need to find a particular piece of information, rather than the general meaning of a text. We move our eyes quickly over the whole text until they focus on the key words that locate the detail we are looking for. This type of reading is called **scanning**. You might, for example, scan a TV guide to find details of a particular programme. You could also look at a bus timetable to find the time of a bus that suits your needs.

> **Key terms**
>
> **Scanning:** reading a text quickly to pick out specific details.

Activity

3

a Text E is taken from a holiday brochure. It describes the Hotel Majestic in Blackpool, the resort and things to do whilst on holiday. Scan Text E on page 6 to see how quickly you can find the answers to the following questions. The key words in each question are in bold.

- How many **stars** does the Hotel Majestic have?
- How might you travel from the Hotel Majestic to the **Pleasure Beach**?
- What can you see from the **viewing platform** of Blackpool Tower?
- What is the name of the **celebrated chef** who works in the hotel?

b Now find the answers to these questions. The key words are no longer in bold.

- Does the hotel have a television in each bedroom?
- Is the Lake District north or south of Blackpool?
- Which village is near Lake Windermere?
- Which cities is Blackpool close to?

Now compare your answers with another student and check the passage if they differ.

The Hotel Majestic, Blackpool

The Hotel Majestic is a three star hotel, found on the North Shore of Blackpool's beautiful bay. The beach is 30 metres from the hotel's main entrance. Hotel Majestic stands in its own grounds, close to the famous North Pier and a short tram ride away from the world famous Pleasure Beach and the night life on the Golden Mile. Within walking distance of the Hotel Majestic is the Sand Castle Leisure Pool where you swim and ride the waves in a glorious tropical setting. A further short walk will take you to Blackpool Tower, where you can take a lift up to the viewing platform and see the magnificent Lancashire coastline and countryside for miles around.

The hotel itself has plenty to offer. In the Tower Restaurant you will enjoy Full English breakfast each morning. For those booking half board, dinner will be cooked by celebrated chef, Nico. For drinks and snacks, you need look no further than the Sandpiper Bar, which offers a wide range of bar meals and fine beers. Rooms at the Majestic are comfortable: each room has its own shower and WC as well as satellite television, hairdryer, towels, trouser press, tea and coffee making facilities.

If you are staying longer in the area you may wish to see some of the sights near to Blackpool. To the north is the picturesque Lake District. A short road journey will take you to Lake Windermere, where you will find wonderful mountain scenery and pretty villages, such as Ambleside. If you prefer shopping to sightseeing, Blackpool is close to the cities of Preston and Lancaster where you will find trendy shops, bars and restaurants.

Signposts

Some texts, for example leaflets, posters and articles, have features such as subheadings, bullet points or bold print to help you find information quickly. These features act like signposts helping you to find your way through a text and locate the key points you are looking for.

- **Subheadings** are used to break up the text into sections. They help you to find what you are looking for quickly by telling you what the section will be about.
- **Bullet points** are used to list important details or information.
- **Bold print** is used to make headings and subheadings stand out and to highlight particular words or phrases for emphasis.

Text F is taken from a leaflet that advises the reader on the use of smoke alarms. It uses subheadings, bullet points and bold print.

Key terms

Subheadings: used to divide text into sections.

Bullet point: used to list details.

Bold print: used to make certain words stand out.

Activity

4 Use the organisational features of Text F to help you find the answers to the following questions:

a What is the minimum number of smoke alarms you should have per floor?

b What should you make sure you do when fitting an alarm?

c What sort of power supply should you choose?

d Why do you need a smoke alarm?

e What different things should you do to make sure your smoke alarm is working properly?

f Where is the best place to position an alarm if you live in a two-storey house?

Check your answers with another student. Where your answers differ, check the text to find out who is right.

Smoke alarms

You are more than twice as likely to die in a fire at home if you haven't got a smoke alarm. A smoke alarm is the easiest way to alert you to the danger of fire, giving you precious time to escape. They are cheap, easy to get hold of and easy to fit.

How many do you need?

The more alarms you have, the safer you'll be. At minimum you should have one on each floor. However, if you have only one alarm and two floors, put it somewhere you'll be able to hear it when you're asleep.

If you have a TV or other large electrical appliance (such as a computer) in any of the bedrooms, you should fit a smoke alarm there too.

The different models available

A lot of people forget to check their smoke alarms, so the best choice of power supply is usually the one that lasts longest.

Installing your smoke alarm

Installing a smoke alarm only takes a few minutes – just follow the manufacturer's instructions that come with it. The best place is on the ceiling, ear or at the middle of the room or hall. The alarm should be at least 30 cm (one foot) away from a wall or light.

If it's difficult for you to fit yourself, ask a family member or friend to help you, or contact your local fire service.

Maintaining your smoke alarm

To keep your smoke alarm in good working order, you should:

- test it once a week, by pressing the test button until the alarm sounds
- change the battery once a year (unless it's a ten-year alarm)
- replace the whole unit every ten years.

You have seen how text marking, skimming, scanning and using organisational features such as topic sentences, bullet points and bold print can help you to find appropriate information in texts to answer specific questions. Now you are going to practise what you have learned.

Check your learning

Re-read Text F. (If you have a copy of the text you can mark and annotate it.)

Identify the methods used to signpost the information by doing the following:

- List two subheadings.
- Look for a paragraph that has a clear topic sentence. Write it down.
- Explain how and why bullet points are used in this text.
- Write down an example of bold print being used to emphasise a point.

2 Making an impact

Objectives

In this chapter you will:

examine how texts are organised

think about how texts are presented to attract and influence the reader.

Purpose and audience

Text A shows the front of a leaflet advertising a theatre production of *An Inspector Calls*. This leaflet has been created by a writer and a graphic designer. Their first task would be to work out the intended purpose and the intended audience for the text.

- The **purpose** of a text is the reason why it was produced. This reason could be, for example, to advise, persuade or entertain.
- The **audience** for a text is the reader for whom it is produced.

Texts sometimes have more than one intended purpose and more than one intended audience.

Key terms

Purpose: the reason why the text has been written – for example to inform or entertain.

Audience: an author writes with a particular person or group of people in mind: this is the intended audience.

Look closely at Text A. The design team wanted the front cover to reflect the following purposes:

- To make people aware of the play.
- To let people know what kind of play it is.
- To suggest how good this production of the play is.
- To link this play to other successful productions.
- To let people know how to find out more information.
- To create an atmosphere or mood of mystery.

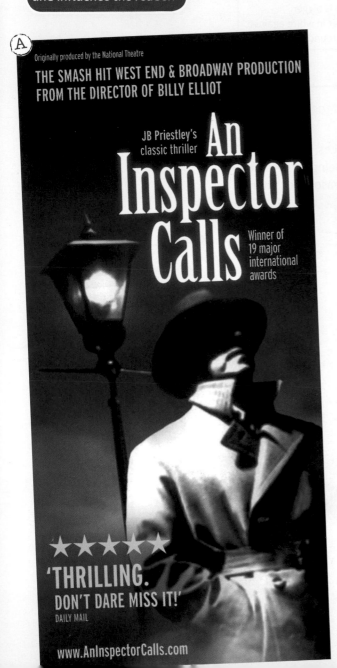

A

Originally produced by the National Theatre

THE SMASH HIT WEST END & BROADWAY PRODUCTION FROM THE DIRECTOR OF BILLY ELLIOT

JB Priestley's classic thriller **An Inspector Calls**

Winner of 19 major international awards

★★★★★ 'THRILLING. DON'T DARE MISS IT!' DAILY MAIL

www.AnInspectorCalls.com

Activities

1 With a partner, copy and complete the following table by finding examples in Text A to show how the design team has tried to meet each of the purposes in the bullet list above. An example is given to help you get started.

Share your ideas with another pair and amend or add to your notes if necessary.

Purpose	Examples
To make people aware of the play	• It mentions the National Theatre, which informs the reader that it is about a play • The play's title stands out very clearly • The font size is bigger • The font is set in white against a dark background
To let people know what kind of play it is	

The design team also had to consider the intended audience for this leaflet.

2 Look at the following list of possible audiences. With a partner, decide which of them you think is being targeted by Text A. Keep a record of your ideas, giving reasons for your choices.

- People who are interested in thrillers or mysteries.
- Fans of romantic comedies.
- Regular theatre-goers.
- Lovers of musicals.
- Students who are studying the play.
- People who are looking for an evening's entertainment.
- Fans of a particular writer, director or theatre company.
- People who appreciate 'quality' productions.
- Primary school children.

Share your ideas with another pair.

Form and features

The design team also need to think about the **form** a text will take. In the case of Text A, it is a leaflet. To encourage someone to take the time to read a leaflet in detail, it needs to stand out from the rest. Designers need to think carefully about:

- pictures
- colours
- words
- print styles/fonts.

Pictures and colours

Pictures and colours are important in creating an initial impact on an audience. They can be used to:

- create a particular **mood** or **atmosphere**
- provide clues to suggest what the leaflet is about
- make one leaflet stand out from the rest.

Key terms

Form: refers to the way text is structured and organised on the page.

Atmosphere/mood: used to describe the feelings or emotions suggested by a text – for example threatening, romantic, tense, etc.

Activity

3 Copy and complete the following table by listing your ideas about how pictures and colours are used in Text A. The column headed 'Prompts' will suggest what you should look at. Some thoughts have already been included to help you get started.

Share your ideas with another pair and amend or add to your notes if necessary.

Feature	Prompts	Thoughts and ideas
Pictures	Think about the camera angle that is used	Low angle shot suggests the man is important, powerful/threatening
	Consider the way the man is dressed	
	Look at the way the man is standing	
	Consider the type of street light	
	Look at the use of shadow	
	Think about the overall impact	
Use of colour	What do you associate with the colours white, gold and dark blue?	The colour gold is often associated with wealth, luxury and quality. In this case, gold is used to highlight the words that suggest this is an outstanding production of high quality. The dark blue …
	How do the colours work when combined together?	
	Think about the overall impact	

Words and fonts

The choice of words clearly has a big impact on the way that people will react or respond to the intended message of the text. The way the words look (for example, the choice of font, its size and shape) can also make a contribution to the impact of a text. The appearance of the words is often referred to as **text style**.

Activity

4 Copy and complete the following table by listing your ideas about the way that words and text styles are used in Text A. The column headed 'Prompts' will suggest what you should look at. Some thoughts have already been included to help you get started.

Share your ideas with another pair and amend or add to your notes if necessary.

Feature	Prompts	Thoughts and ideas
Words	Consider the use of these words • Smash hit	'Smash hit' suggests that this is a very popular production and therefore should not be missed
	• West End and Broadway production	
	• Classic thriller	
	• 19 major international awards	
	• Thrilling	
	• Don't dare miss it	
Text styles	How are capital letters used?	The size of the font used for the words *An Inspector Calls* means that the title dominates the page. It is probably the first thing you notice on the leaflet …
	How and where are capital letters used?	
	Think about the overall impact	
	Which words are in the smallest font? Why?	

Key terms

Text style: the way the words look – for example, choice of font, size and shape.

Writing about features

When writing about **features** of language and presentation, you need to assess their **impact** and **effect** on the reader. To do this, you need to:

- identify the features
- explain how and why they have been used.

Text B is taken from one student's written response to the front page of Text A. The paragraph has been highlighted in two different colours:

- Green to show the student identifying a feature.
- Yellow to show the student explaining how and why a feature has been used.

Key terms

Feature: something about a text that you can comment on – for example, features of a leaflet might be the layout, the language used or the colours used.

Impact: the reaction that an audience has to a feature or features of a text.

Effect: what the audience feels or does as a result of seeing the text.

B

When you see the leaflet, the first thing you notice is the title of the play, 'An Inspector Calls'. It is written in a large font and, because it is white, it stands out against the dark-blue background. The overall darkness could suggest that things are hidden or out of sight and that the Inspector's task is to uncover them. Darkness and the night time feel of the colour reinforce the possibility of threat and mystery. The use of gold is also important. Gold is often associated with wealth, luxury and quality. In this case, gold is used to highlight the words that suggest this is an outstanding production of high quality.

Activities

5 In Text C, the same student has written about the use of pictures in Text A. Copy out the paragraph and use two colours to highlight:

- where the student identifies features of the text
- where the student explains how and why the features have been used.

C

The image of the inspector is shot from a low angle. This means he appears big and powerful, even a little threatening or mysterious. He is a man to be respected or to fear. He is dressed very formally, but in an old-fashioned way with a hat and overcoat. This makes him seem very important and also tells us that this play is not set in modern times. The fact that he is lit by a gas lamp casts shadows and adds to the mystery. We cannot see his face clearly.

6 **a** Use the table you made in Activity 4 to help you write a short paragraph explaining how words and fonts have been used in Text A and why.

b Work with a partner to assess how well you have completed Activity 6a. Look at the paragraphs you each wrote and use two colours to highlight:

- where you have identified features
- where you have explained how and why the features have been used.

Discuss with your partner how you could have developed and improved your explanations.

'STEPHEN DALDRY'S THRILLING AWARD-LADEN PRODUCTION HAS RETURNED. The defining production of the 1990s, a work of great directorial daring, breathtaking visual invention and passionate moral urgency.'
DAILY TELEGRAPH

'STUNNING. Blazingly original stage imagery. Dark and gleaming and elegant'
NEW YORK TIMES

'URGENT & THRILLING. Spine-tinglingly good. Grabs you by the throat. Long may it do so'
THE GUARDIAN

JB Priestley's classic thriller **An Inspector Calls**

Director STEPHEN DALDRY
Designer IAN MacNEIL
Lighting Designer RICK FISHER
Music STEPHEN WARBECK
Associate Director JULIAN WEBBER

From the Director of the Academy Award-winning blockbuster The Hours and one of Britain's best-loved films Billy Elliot - now an Olivier Award-winning musical - comes the smash hit West End & Broadway production of JB Priestley's classic thriller, An Inspector Calls.

Hailed as the theatrical event of our generation winning more awards than any other play in history, this magnificent production has thrilled audiences across the world with its epic and wildly imaginative staging, raw emotion, evocative score, lashing rain and searing suspense.

When Inspector Goole arrives unexpectedly at the prosperous Birling family home, their peaceful dinner party is shattered by his investigations into the death of a young woman. His startling revelations shake the very foundations of their lives and challenge us all to examine our consciences.

'OUTSTANDING. A genuinely great production, enthralling and visually stunning'
DAILY TELEGRAPH

Check your learning

Use the skills you have developed in this chapter to examine another part of the leaflet (Text D). Follow these steps:

a Identify and make notes about how colours have been used and why.

b Identify and make notes about how images have been used and why.

c Make notes on the impact and effect of these on the intended reader.

d Write two paragraphs in which you identify and explain the features.

e Re-read your paragraphs and use two colours to highlight:

- the features you have identified
- your explanations of them.

3 Engaging stories

Objectives

In this chapter you will:

read a variety of texts

examine how writers use words to create character, setting and mood

learn how to develop comments on details in a text.

In this chapter, you will learn how writers use a variety of words and phrases to affect the way the reader thinks about and reacts to what the writer has written. Writers decide how to use characters, **dialogue**, **setting**, events and situations, and *mood* to make the reader feel the way they want them to.

Key terms

Dialogue: words that are spoken by characters.

Setting: place or places where the story happens.

Characters

Writers create characters. They decide their appearance, their actions, their words, what other characters think about them and what happens to them. The reader needs to use the details given to help them understand and respond to the characters.

Read these opening sentences (Text A) from an extract in which the writer introduces the character Seth Thompson to the reader. The text markings highlight things to notice.

(A)

Seth Thompson was a tough man. He ran his business with a rod of iron. Every day he patrolled his factory like a prison warder, looking for the slightest sign that someone might be slacking. There was no laughter, no sense of fun, nothing to suggest anyone enjoyed their job. Workers did not dare to look up from their benches for fear of catching his eye. They worked like slaves.

Reinforces the first impression of 'toughness'

He spends his time looking for trouble

The simile shows just how hard the work is

The first adjective used to describe him

The simile compares him directly with a prison warder

The group of three emphasises the misery of the workers

The workers are afraid of him

15

1

a Now read and copy the rest of the paragraph about Seth Thompson (Text B). Highlight and make notes on the details that tell you more about him.

b Consider what you have learnt about Seth Thompson from the whole of the paragraph. In one or two sentences, explain **what** you think of him and **why** you think this.

> Seth Thompson never smiled and he rarely spoke. He strutted, walking miles every day, up and down the factory floor, searching for faults. When he did pass comment, he rarely wasted words and he spoke in commands: 'Pick that up!' or 'That's rubbish, lad. Do it again!' Experienced hands were quietly resentful of his words; young workers were terrified.

Dialogue

As you probably noticed when answering Activity 1a, writers often reveal character through:

- the words that are spoken
- the way the words are spoken.

We are told the words Seth speaks but also that he 'spoke in commands'. This gives the reader a clear idea of the tone of his voice.

In scripts for plays, writers sometimes give actors directions as to how words should be spoken.

Text C is taken from the script of the play *Blood Brothers* by Willy Russell. Mickey and Edward are two seven-year-old boys. They are twins who were separated at birth. In this extract they meet, by chance, for the first time.

Activity

2

a Read Text C and, under two separate headings, 'Mickey' and 'Edward', make notes on what you learn about them from the things they say and the way they say them.

b Now read what one student wrote about Edward (Text D). The details taken from the passage are highlighted in blue. The student's own comments on the details are highlighted in pink.

Blood Brothers

Mickey (*suspiciously*): Hello.

Edward: I've seen you before.

Mickey: Where?

Edward: You were playing with some other boys near my house.

Mickey: Do you live up in the park?

Edward: Yes. Are you going to come and play up there again?

Mickey: No. I would do but I'm not allowed.

Edward: Why?

Mickey: 'Cos me mam says.

Edward: Well, my mummy doesn't allow me to play down here actually.

Mickey: 'Gis a sweet.

Edward: All right. (*He offers a bag from his pocket*)

Mickey (*shocked*): What?

Edward: Here.

Mickey (*trying to work out the catch. Suspiciously taking one*): Can I have another one. For our Sammy?

Edward: Yes, of course. Take as many as you want.

Mickey (*taking a handful*): Are you soft?

Edward: I don't think so.

Mickey: Round here if y' ask for a sweet, y'have to ask about, about twenty million times. An' y' know what?

Edward (*sitting beside Mickey*): What?

Mickey: They still don't bleedin' give y' one. Sometimes our Sammy does but y' have to be dead careful if our Sammy gives y' a sweet.

Edward: Why?

Mickey: 'Cos, if our Sammy gives y' a sweet he's usually weed on it first.

Willy Russell, *Blood Brothers,* Methuen Drama, 1983

The way Edward talks sounds like he is from a well-off family. He says 'mummy' instead of 'mum' or, like Mickey says, 'mam'. He sounds formal and uses words like 'actually' when he speaks, which all suggest that he speaks properly. It sounds as though he might be over protected as he's not allowed to go to the park. He is happy to share his sweets, which makes the reader think that treats are common in his house and that sharing is expected. He might be lonely as he seems anxious to make friends.

Notice how the student is using the details to work out or infer things. This is sometimes called inference and shows that the student is thinking about and interpreting what he has read.

Activity

3 Look back at the notes you made in Activity 2. Write a paragraph showing what you learn about Mickey from:

- what he says about his family
- how he reacts to Edward's offer of a sweet
- the way he speaks.

Remember to use details from the extract and to comment on the details you use.

Setting

Writers often create a very clear picture of the place or places where a story happens. This is called the setting. In Text E, Dickens describes a school.

Activity

4 **a** Read Text E from *Nicholas Nickleby* by Charles Dickens. Pick out and list six details that tell you something about the school Dickens is describing.

b Which of the following phrases do you think best describes the school?

- The school is busy and well looked after.
- The school is a good place in which to learn.
- The school is run down and in need of repair.

Nicholas Nickleby

'There,' said the schoolmaster as they stepped in together; 'this is our shop, Nickleby!'

It was such a crowded scene, and there were so many objects to attract attention, that, at first, Nicholas stared about him, really without seeing anything at all. By degrees, however, the place resolved itself into a bare and dirty room, with a couple of windows, whereof a tenth part might be of glass, the remainder being stopped up with old copy-books and paper. There were a couple of long old rickety desks, cut and notched, and inked, and damaged, in every possible way … The ceiling was supported, like that of a barn, by cross-beams and rafters; and the walls were so stained and discoloured, that it was impossible to tell whether they had ever been touched with paint or whitewash.

Charles Dickens, *Nicholas Nickleby*, 1839

Now read Text F, written about the school by a student, based on the information about the setting in the extract. Again, you can see how the student has used details from the passage (highlighted in blue) and made comments or inferences on these (highlighted in pink).

(F) The highlighted words and phrases build up the reader's idea of what the classroom is like. The place is described as 'crowded', 'dirty' and generally run down. Words like 'rickety', 'stained' and 'discoloured' mean that it needs to be redecorated and repaired. The writer suggests that the windows are in such a poor state that only 'a tenth part might be of glass', which means that the windows must have been broken and not fixed properly. Such a dull and dismal place that does not seem like a good place to learn.

Activity

5

a Now it's your turn. Carefully read the extract from *Oliver Twist* (Text G), which describes market day in London.

With a partner, list words and phrases that help you to imagine:
- what you would see on market morning
- what you would hear on market morning.

b Think about the phrase 'the reeking bodies of the cattle'. What is the writer suggesting by the use of the adjective 'reeking' in this phrase?

c Re-read the second paragraph on your own and write a paragraph to explain how Dickens uses words to describe the sounds of a market morning. Remember to:
- use detail from the passage
- comment on the detail you use.

d Swap your writing with your partner. Using two colours:
- highlight the detail taken from the passage
- the comments made on this detail.

(G)

Oliver Twist

It was market-morning. The ground was covered, nearly ankle-deep, with filth and mire; a thick steam, perpetually rising from the reeking bodies of the cattle, and mingling with the fog, which seemed to rest upon the chimney-tops, hung heavily above. All the pens in the centre of the large area, and as many temporary pens as could be crowded into the vacant space, were filled with sheep; tied up to the posts by the gutter side were long lines of beasts and oxen, three or four deep.

Countrymen, butchers, drovers, hawkers, boys, thieves, idlers and vagabonds of every low grade, were mingled together in a mass; the whistling of drovers, the barking of dogs, the bellowing and plunging of oxen, the bleating of sheep, the grunting and squeaking of pigs, the cries of hawkers, the shouts, oaths and quarrelling on all sides, whooping and yelling; the hideous and discordant din that resounded from every corner of the market; and the unwashed, unshaven, squalid, and dirty figures constantly running to and fro, and bursting in and out of the throng, rendered it a stunning and bewildering scene that quite confounded the senses.

Charles Dickens, *Oliver Twist*, 1838

Creating mood

Mood is another name for the atmosphere or feeling that is created in a text – for example, the mood could be frightening, mysterious, cheerful, threatening, etc. In a film, music might be used to create mood. In writing, authors use words. Text H is the opening of a short story.

You are going to examine how the writer uses words to create mood and atmosphere in this story opening.

The building stood, alone and threatening on the distant peak. The once famous hotel was now cloaked by trees, and choked by vines, its shattered windows glowering at the valley below. The sun had long since shrunk into the west but the crescent moon dared not show its face tonight. All was silent. All was still.

Activity

6

a Copy and complete the following table showing what is suggested by the writer's choice of words in Text H. The first and the last rows have been done as examples, but you may want to add to them.

alone and threatening	'alone' makes us realise that there are no other buildings there and 'threatening' suggests the place is dangerous in some way.
distant peak	
once famous	
cloaked by trees	
choked by vines	
shattered windows	
glowering	
shrunk	
dared not	
All was silent. All was still.	The repetition emphasises the quiet and lack of movement. It suggests that something is about to happen to change this.

b Choose two or three adjectives that describe the mood or atmosphere the writer creates in this opening paragraph.

c By using different words, a writer can create a very different mood or atmosphere, for example:

> proud and welcoming   gently sloping hill
> The building stood, ~~alone and threatening~~, on the ~~distant peak~~.

Rewrite the rest of the opening paragraph shown in Text H. Aim to create a lively, happy mood through your choice of words.

d Compare your writing in Activity 6c with another student. Decide which of you has been the most successful in choosing words to create a lively, happy mood.

Creating tone

A writer can adopt a number of different tones when writing. For example, they may use a sarcastic tone, an angry tone, a cheerful and lively tone, a pessimistic tone, or a friendly tone. This will depend on the effect they want to have on the reader.

Read Text I taken from an advertisement for a hotel.

Key terms

Tone: a writer's attitude towards the subject and/or audience – for example, serious, humorous, angry or sad.

The Park Hotel ★ ★ ★ ★

The Park Hotel, Park Road, Cheshire, CH1 4XP
Tel: 01876 65234 Fax: 01876 737876
Email: parkroyal@qhotels.co.uk

The Park Hotel is a hidden treasure in a beautiful setting. There's the stunning Cheshire countryside, quaint villages, meandering rivers and picturesque canals – plus the buzz of the city too! With extensive boutique shopping, Chester caters for every fashion whim.

Once inside your en-suite room you'll feel more relaxed in seconds, surrounded by every modern convenience. Our 85 recently refurbished bedrooms have all the amenities you might expect: mini-bar, satellite TV, tea, coffee and telephone. Choose the Balmoral Suite and you even have your own hot tub and balcony. And, if you want to arrive by helicopter, we have our own helipad in the grounds!

As for things to do in the area? Aintree, perhaps, or the North Wales coastline, Chester Zoo, the Gateway Theatre, Beeston Castle, Chester has something for everyone! The list is endless – there's even an evening of ghost hunting.

The Park Hotel ★ ★ ★ ★

Activity

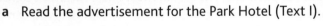

7

a Read the advertisement for the Park Hotel (Text I).

It tells the reader about:

- the hotel's setting
- the hotel's facilities
- things to do in the local area.

Find and write down words and details in the text that are intended to make each of these things appealing to the reader.

b How many times does the writer address the reader directly? What is the intended effect of this on the reader?

c In pairs, discuss which words you would use to describe the overall tone of the advertisement. Take one paragraph and experiment with changing the words in order to change the tone.

Check your learning

In this chapter, you have explored the ways in which writers make deliberate choices of words to:

- interest and
- influence

the reader's response to the text.

Use what you have learned to help you write one paragraph explaining how the writer of Text I has used words to influence the reader. Remember to:

- refer to the words in the text
- comment on the use of words.

4

Objectives

In this chapter you will:

build on what you have learnt in Chapters 2 and 3

think about the effectiveness of features of presentation and language

learn about evaluation

write an evaluation.

Evaluating texts

When you **evaluate** something, you make a series of judgements on it based on evidence.

To evaluate a text, you need to think about:

- the intended **audience(s)** of the text (the group of people it was written for, such as teenaged girls, middle-aged men, or sports fans)
- the **purpose(s)** of the text (these could be to inform, advise, entertain, etc.)
- the use of **presentational features** (such as pictures, colours, fonts, captions, graphs)
- the use of **language** (such as **vocabulary**, sentence variety).

Key terms

Evaluate: to make a judgement on something based on evidence.

Vocabulary: words used in a text, which are chosen to have an impact on the reader.

Purpose and audience 🕪

Remember that authors write with a particular purpose and audience in mind. For example, an election leaflet might be intended to **inform** readers about policies and **persuade** them to vote for a particular party. It is also likely to be aimed at an **adult audience**. A magazine advert for fashionable jeans is likely to be intended to **persuade** readers to buy the product and is likely to target **teenagers** and **young adults**.

Activity

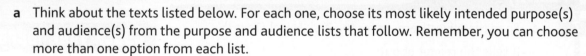

1

a Think about the texts listed below. For each one, choose its most likely intended purpose(s) and audience(s) from the purpose and audience lists that follow. Remember, you can choose more than one option from each list.

Texts:

- a fairy tale
- leaflet about applying for college
- advertisement for a sports car
- article about the dangers of drinking
- advertisement for fishing rods
- dating webpage.

Possible purposes: to inform, to argue, to persuade, to entertain, to advise, to explain.

Possible audiences: male/female/pensioners/parents/young adults/teenagers/children/ people interested in something specific.

b Compare your choices with another student and discuss the reasons for any differences.

Presentation and language

In Chapter 2, you learnt about how writers and designers adapt the appearance of a text to achieve their intended purpose(s) and influence their intended audience(s). To do this, they use a range of presentational features such as pictures, colours, headlines and subheadings.

In Chapter 3, you learnt how writers use words to achieve their intended purpose(s) and influence their intended audience(s).

They might use language formally or informally, choose particular phrases to describe something or to create mood and atmosphere, or target their reader directly through the use of the second person (you).

A writer's use of language and a designer's use of presentational features are adapted to their purpose(s) and audience(s).

Activity

2 Study Texts A and B below. Match the appropriate use of features of presentation and language from the list below to each text:

- picture that reflects the story
- simple sentences
- large print
- short sentences for effect
- repetition for effect
- language to persuade
- bright colours
- picture of the product
- use of the second person (you)
- simple vocabulary
- complex sentences
- technical vocabulary.

(B) The new Phenon laptop is at the cutting edge of modern computer technology. It comes with 4MB of RAM memory as standard and a massive 250GB hard drive, enough to allow you to surf and download music and films to your heart's content. The Phenon is a compact and slim laptop, weighing only 2 kilograms, so it will not slow you down on the way to or from your next meeting and will fit snugly into a small bag. With full wi-fi capability, you will be able to access your e-mails or Facebook wherever in the world you happen to visit. The graphics card is a Xenon XB24 and will allow games fans to play even the most demanding games online. With a battery life of 8 hours, you will have plenty of power if you are away from home for long periods of time.

At £499 it is not the cheapest around, but, if you want quality, this is a bargain. Buy one today!

With a partner, discuss:

- the intended purpose(s) and audience(s) of Texts A and B
- whether you think the presentational features and use of language have been successfully matched to purpose and audience.

Evaluation: making a judgement

In Activity 3 you made a judgement on how successful the writers and designers of Texts A and B were in using language and presentation to suit purpose and audience. In making that judgement, you were evaluating the text.

When you are asked to evaluate something, you are being asked for **your opinion.** There is no single correct answer, though it is important to give clear reasons for your opinion based on evidence in the text. Remember, you are not judging the subject of the text; you are evaluating how well it achieves its purpose and matches its audience.

With a partner, look closely at Text C, which is a poster for the suspense thriller, *Panic Room*. Copy and complete the table below to identify:

- the main presentational features and their effect(s)
- the impact you think they would have on the intended purpose(s) and audience(s).

Share your findings with another pair. Compare what you have written and add to your table if appropriate.

Presentational features	Comments on the effects of the presentational features	Targeted purpose(s) and audience(s)	Likely impact of the presentational features on the targeted purpose(s) and audience(s)

Writing an evaluation about presentational features 🔵 k!

You could use the notes you made in the table in Activity 4 to help you to write an answer to the following question:

'The presentational features used in the poster for *Panic Room* are intended to attract people to watch the film. How likely are they to succeed?'

Read the following opening paragraphs from a student's response to this question (Text D). The student's response has been annotated by a teacher to show you what information they have used to evaluate the text.

Identifies potential audience

Identifies possible purposes

Supporting evidence

Ⓓ The poster is aimed at young adults who might like to be shocked or frightened by what they see on the screen. Its main purpose is to create a sense of suspense and threat to persuade the audience that the film is worth seeing which is suggested by the fearful expression on the actress's face.

The two main colours, black and red, are often associated with horror, danger, death and bloodshed. These are intended to introduce these ideas to the audience so that they have a clear idea of what to expect if they see the film. They would almost certainly attract fans of thriller movies as they promise an evening of twists and turns to keep the viewer on the edge of his or her seat.

Identifies presentational features

Comments on why the feature is used

Makes a judgement

Supports judgement with a reason

Activity

5 With a partner, read Text E, a response written by the same student who wrote Text D. If you have a copy of the student's answer, you could highlight or underline the words in the text and make notes in the margin. Otherwise, you could record your notes in a table like the one below. Find and make a note of one example of each of the following features:

- talks about intended purpose
- talks about intended audience
- identifies features of presentation
- comments on why these features are used
- offers a personal opinion.

- supports comments with evidence from the text
- makes a judgement
- supports their judgement with reasons

Feature	Example from student's writing
Talks about intended purpose	
Talks about intended audience	

E The still photograph on the poster has been taken from low down and focuses on the eyes of the actress. This has been done for two reasons. The first is to show the look of shock and fear in the woman's eyes. The other is to show a tall, threatening figure of a man towering above her. This type of shot is likely to work well on the target audience, which is likely to be fans of horror and suspense films. It makes them want to watch the film to find out why she is in this situation, who the man is and what he wants from her.

She seems to be lying down, which makes her look more vulnerable. Her expression is clearly visible, whereas the man is standing in shadow making him seem suspicious and mysterious. The image does not actually fill the page and has been made narrow so that it seems as though the viewer is looking on and observing her fear from the outside. These features work well together to make the film appealing to its potential audience because they create suspense and a threatening atmosphere. Personally, I would want to find out if and how she escapes from the situation.

Writing an evaluation about language 🗨️

Sometimes you might be asked to evaluate the writer's use of language.

Read Text F, which is taken from a letter. The **intended purpose** is to persuade the readers that they should support this charity. The intended **audience** is readers who may be interested in making a contribution to the charity. Some of the writer's language choices have been identified for you.

F Dear Helper,

Thank you for sending off for this pack. You are already well on the way to helping others.

Personal – involves the reader from the start

Earlier this year, I took some time out to visit Africa to see some of the work that has been completed since the last appeal. I went to Namibia and there I met Kara. The last time I saw her she was a badly undernourished, vulnerable nine-year-old girl forced to walk three miles a day across rocky, barren, desert roads to fetch water for her family. Then she would carry it back to the village in a stone pot. It was back-breaking work. Today, all that has changed. Due to our work, Kara's village now has its own water pipe and she has only to walk 50 metres from her house to fill up her stone jar. Now she attends school and has dreams of becoming a doctor to help the very many sick people in her country.

This story helps the reader think of real people being helped

Emotive use of language to appeal to the reader's feelings

However, success stories such as this one are all too rare. We still have lots to do if we are to wipe out poverty, disease and hunger in this world. How could anyone refuse such a challenge? I know that you will not let others down. You have already taken the first step by sending for this pack.

Rule of three – emphasises how great the challenge is

Personal – encourages the reader to help

Rhetorical question used to persuade the reader to accept the challenge

6 Read the following two paragraphs from the same letter (Text G). Identify and comment on the effects of the use of:

- facts
- emotive language
- rule of three
- real-life stories/anecdotes
- first-person singular and plural (I, we)
- rhetorical question
- humour.

Either highlight and annotate a copy of the paragraphs or record your notes in a table like the one below.

Language	Example from text	Likely effect on reader
Use of facts		
Emotive language		

G

We have made a difference to thousands of lives in the last two years. We have completed 75 projects in this country alone and 190 abroad. This means that many people, often children and babies, are healthier, safer and more secure than it was ever thought possible. But there are still millions living in poverty who need your help. There are many fellow humans who have nowhere to sleep, little food and just as many who are orphans. In Cambodia, I saw children as young as five begging for food on the street. They were undernourished and alone. In their eyes you could see the suffering they had been through. I thought of my own children and realised how lucky they and we all are in Britain.

So now it is time for us to help those children and as many of the others as we can. What better way to do it than having fun? So, get your friends organised. Sit in a bath of custard, get yourself sponsored to kiss your Aunt Ethel or to eat cabbages, sponsor your teachers to teach an interesting lesson for a change! Anything will do. Just get out there and make a difference. Little Kara and those Cambodian children will thank you for life. Literally!

Check your learning

Remind yourself of the intended purpose and audience of this letter, given on page 27. Use the notes you have made to help you write an answer to the following question:

How successful is the writer in using language to persuade the readers to support this charity?

Before you write your answer look back at the student's written evaluation on pages 26 and 27.

Remember to:

- refer to purpose, audience
- give your opinions on the effectiveness of the different uses of language
- support your opinions with reference to examples in the text.

Aim to write two or three developed paragraphs.

The time and the place

Objectives

In this chapter you will:

learn how texts are often shaped by the time in history when they were written

learn how the culture or the kind of society in which the writer lives can affect what they write.

Background

When you first read a text, it is often without knowing anything of the background of the writer or the time or place about which it is written. In this chapter, you will discover how finding out more about the background can help you to develop a better understanding of a text.

Texts in time

When you read a text, you need to consider the time in which it was written. All languages change over time in the words that are used, the spellings of words and the order in which the words are written or spoken. When you first read a text, the language may seem unfamiliar to you and require extra effort to understand it.

Activity

1

a The following lines are taken from texts written in different centuries. Try to place them in the correct chronological order with the oldest one first.

'Nor sporting in the dalliance of love'

'I was all right on the Monday. I was all right on the Tuesday. And I was all right on the Wednesday until lunchtime, at which point all my nice little routine went out the window.'

'My dear Algy, you talk exactly as if you were a dentist. It is very vulgar to talk like a dentist when one isn't a dentist. It produces a false impression ...'

'A rose gerland, fressh and wel smellynge'

b Compare your order with another student. Discuss:

- any differences you may have
- what clues you used to decide your order
- when you think the texts were written.

c Check your order with the correct order given at the end of this chapter.

It is not just the words that present a challenge when we read a text written from an earlier time. Often, they refer to things that were relevant to the time in which they were written.

Read Text A from *Oliver Twist,* which was written by Charles Dickens in 1837. It focuses on a small orphan boy who grew up in the workhouse system of the time. Note that the 'they' referred to in the extract are the officials of the workhouse.

With this view, they contracted with the waterworks to lay on an unlimited supply of water, and with a corn-factor to supply periodically small quantities of oatmeal; and issued three meals of thin gruel a day, with an onion twice a week, and a half a roll on Sundays.

(The board also)

… kindly undertook to divorce poor married couples, in consequence of the great expense of a suit in the Doctors' Commons; and instead of compelling a man to support his family as they had theretofore done, took his family away from him, and made him a bachelor!

Charles Dickens, Oliver Twist, 1838

Activity

2   With a partner, spend a couple of minutes discussing what you think:

- the paragraphs are about
- what Dickens' purpose was writing these paragraphs.

Did you find Activity 2 difficult? It is hard to know what the writer's purpose was because we do not have enough information. Read Text B, which gives an explanation of the workhouse system and see how this helps to explain the purpose.

The workhouse system was set up in England and Wales in 1834. It was designed to provide relief for the needy. However, concerns that too many people would take advantage of the system led to the introduction of a harsh and degrading routine. Men, women and children were separated and inmates were forced to wear a distinctive uniform. In many ways, the workhouse was like a prison and many inmates felt they were being punished for the crime of poverty. Charles Dickens, whose own childhood was hit by poverty, aimed to expose the workhouse regime for what it truly was.

Activity

3   In the same pairs, use the information you have learned from Text B to think again about Dickens' purpose. What was he showing the reader about the workhouse system?

Knowing a bit more about the time in which the novel was written and the aspect that Dickens' was writing about (workhouses), makes it easier to work out the writer's purpose.

Texts and attitudes

As you have seen, texts can often reveal things about a particular time. In this chapter you are going to examine two advertisements produced within 60 years of each other. The first (Text C) was published in the 1950s and the second (Text D) in the 21st century. Both texts reveal things about attitudes to women. By comparing the two texts, you can see how these attitudes have changed.

Activity

4

a With a partner, look first at the picture in the Listerine advertisement (Text C).

Discuss and write your answers to the following questions:

i What do you notice about the way the woman is dressed?

ii Look at the woman's facial expression, body language and where she is standing. What do these tell you about the woman and the purpose of the advertisement?

b Now read the words in the advertisement. Discuss and write your answers to the following questions:

i Who is the intended audience of the advertisement? Give a reason for your answer.

ii Think about the following phrases. What do they suggest will happen to a woman who does not use Listerine?

- 'She's popular with the girls …'
- '… attractive to men for a while.'
- 'Men seem serious – then just courteous – finally, oblivious.'
- 'Halitosis is a roadblock to romance.'
- '… you're never aware that you're offending!'

c Now think about the picture and the words. Discuss:

- what this advertisement suggests to you about the role of women and what they expected from life in the 1950s
- how you feel about the images of the woman given in the advertisement.

Often a bridesmaid…
never a bride!

Janice is a familiar type. She's popular with the girls … attractive to men *for a while*. Men seem serious— then just courteous—finally, oblivious. Halitosis (unpleasant breath) is a roadblock to romance. And the tragedy is, you're never aware that you're offending!

The most common cause of bad breath is germs …
Listerine kills germs by millions

And why should anyone risk halitosis when Listerine Antiseptic ends it so quickly? Germs—which ferment the proteins always present in your mouth—are the most common cause of bad breath. The more you reduce these germs, the longer your breath stays sweeter. Listerine kills germs on contact … by millions.

Tooth paste can't kill germs the way Listerine does

Tooth paste can't kill germs the way Listerine does, because no tooth paste is antiseptic. Listerine IS antiseptic. That's why Listerine stops bad breath four times better than tooth paste. Gargle Listerine full-strength every morning, every night, before every date!

THE MOST WIDELY USED
ANTISEPTIC IN THE WORLD!

LISTERINE ANTISEPTIC…STOPS BAD BREATH
4 times better than tooth paste

Now read the advertisement published in 2001 in Text D.

www.suzuki.co.uk

confidence ign**is**

all about how you carry yourself

IGNIS

Activity

5 With a partner, discuss and write your answers to the following questions:

a The camera shot is taken from low down, looking up at the woman. How does that make her appear to the reader?

b Think about the way the woman is dressed and the way she is walking. Why do you think she has been photographed in this way?

c Look at the background. What do you think the building might be? Why might she be there?

d What do the words above the car suggest about the woman?

The next step is to use your ideas to write a more developed answer that shows you understand how texts can reflect the attitudes of the time in which they were produced.

Activity

6 What does Text D, the advertisement for Suzuki Ignis, suggest about life for women in the 21st century? Text E shows how one student prepared her answer. Use your own ideas and the student's notes to help you write your own answer. Aim to write one or two developed paragraphs. Remember to refer to details in the text and to develop your opinions.

Ⓔ
Points to make:

- Seems to be coming from her own flat – independent woman?
- Has own car.
- Carrying bag or office diary – own career?
- Dressed casually – confident? Does not have to dress to impress others.
- Camera looking up at her – makes her seem important, confident, in control of her life.

Key words to help me explain points:

- suggests ...
- implies ...
- shows ...
- represents ...
- seems to ...

Texts, places and cultures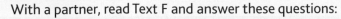

Texts can reveal things about the time in which they were written. They can also reveal things about different places and cultures. Text F is about a West Indian man now living in London. The poet, Grace Nichols, is also from the West Indies.

Activity

7 With a partner, read Text F and answer these questions:

a What different things does the man think about as he starts to wake each morning?

b How would you describe the place he is thinking of in the first two stanzas?

c Which word in the first stanza suggests that this place is the place of his birth?

d Which words in the second stanza suggest that this place is precious to him?

e At which point in the poem does the man's thoughts move from the place of his dreams to the place he now lives in?

f In what ways is London shown to be different from the place of his birth?

g How does the island man seem to feel about where he now lives? Refer to details in the poem to support your points.

h Suggest reasons which would explain why the island man is not given a name.

F

Island Man

*(For a Caribbean man in London who still
wakes up to the sound of the sea)*

Morning
and island man wakes up
to the sound of blue surf
in his head
the steady breaking and wombing

wild seabirds
and fisherman pushing out to sea
the sun surfacing defiantly
from the east
of his small emerald island
he always comes back groggily groggily

Comes back to sands
of a grey metallic soar
to surge of wheels
to dull North Circular roar
muffling muffling

his crumpled pillow waves
island man heaves himself
Another London day

Grace Nichols, 'Island Man'

Key terms

Culture: a set of shared beliefs and values that define a group of people and shape their behaviour and ways of thinking.

Texts in context

The context of a text relates to when and where it was written, and by whom. It is not essential to know the context of a text to read and understand it. However, knowing the context can, sometimes, greatly enhance understanding and appreciation of a text.

8

With a partner, read Text G carefully a few times before thinking about and answering the questions that surround it. Base your answers on evidence given in the poem.

a What do you learn about the past of the person they are moving 'into the sun'?

b How do you know he has just died?

c What is the tone of the first stanza?

d In your own words, explain the questions the poet asks.

e What is the **tone** of the second stanza?

f How does the poet feel about this death?

g How does the content of the poem link with its title?

h What does the poem make you think about and how does it make you feel?

Key terms

Tone: a writer's attitude towards the subject and/or audience – for example, serious, humorous, angry or sad.

(G)

Futility

Move him into the sun –
Gently its touch awoke him once,
At home, whispering of fields unsown.
Always it woke him, even in France,
Until this morning and this snow.
If anything might rouse him now
The kind old sun will know.

Think how it wakes the seeds, –
Woke, once, the clays of a cold star.
Are limbs, so dear-achieved, are sides,
Full-nerved – still warm – too hard to stir?
Was it for this the clay grew tall?
– O what made fatuous sunbeams toil
To break earth's sleep at all?

Wilfred Owen, 'Futility', 1918

Now that you have read and thought about the poem (Text G), you are going to learn more about its context. Read the following information:

- **Historical context**: 'Futility' was written in 1918. It is about a young man who was a soldier and who died fighting for his country, England, in the First World War (1914–18). It was a war in which more than 15 million people were killed.

- **Social context**: At the start of the war, people in England believed it was a great honour to fight and die for their country. As time progressed, however, and they learnt more about the terrible conditions of the war, attitudes started to change.

- **The writer**: Wilfred Owen (1893–1918) is a famous war poet. He enlisted at the age of 22 and experienced dreadful things. These included being blown high into the air by a trench mortar and landing in the remains of a fellow officer. He was sent home to recover from shell shock but chose to return to the front. He was killed in action a week before the war ended.

Activities

9 Re-read 'Futility'. Using what you have learnt about the context, what more can you now say about:

- the man who has died and how he has died
- the tone of the first and second stanzas and the reasons for the differences in tone
- how the poet feels about the man's death
- how the poet feels about war
- why the poet chose the title 'Futility'?

10 Rewrite your answer to the question: What does the poem make you think about and how does it make you feel?

11 Look again at the picture that accompanies Text G. Do you think it is an appropriate reflection of the poem? If you could change it, how would you? Give your reasons.

Answer to Activity 1a

Chronological order of extracts:

'A rose gerland, fressh and wel smellynge' from *The Canterbury Tales: the Knight's Tale* by Geoffrey Chaucer, 1387–1400.

'Nor sporting in the dalliance of love' from *Dr Faustus* by Christopher Marlowe, 1604.

'My dear Algy, you talk exactly as if you were a dentist. It is very vulgar to talk like a dentist when one isn't a dentist. It produces a false impression…' from *The Importance of Being Earnest* by Oscar Wilde, 1895.

'I was all right on the Monday. I was all right on the Tuesday. And I was all right on the Wednesday until lunchtime, at which point all my nice little routine went out the window.' from *Talking Heads* by Alan Bennett, 1987.

Check your learning

With a partner, share your ideas of what each of the following means:

- social context
- historical context
- cultural context.

Creating a story

Objectives

In this chapter you will:

investigate the ways that writers create stories and how they get and keep their readers' attention, focusing on: openings, setting and endings

evaluate the effectiveness of these tools.

A narrative is a story about something. It could be invented, like a fairy tale, or it could be a real-life experience, like an **autobiography**. In this chapter, you will investigate the ways that writers put stories together to get and keep the attention of the reader.

Key terms

Autobiography: the story of a person's life written by him or herself.

Openings

For a writer to engage a reader's interest, the opening to a narrative must be interesting and encourage the reader to continue. There are several ways of starting a story. The examples in this chapter will show you how stories start with action or by introducing a character.

Starting with action

Read Text A, the opening to a story about a car accident called *Crash*. The story is written from the point of view of an outsider. This is called a third-person narrative. Characters in the story are identified as 'she' or 'he' or 'they'. As the narrator is not a character, he or she is able to have an overview of everything that occurs and is thought and felt.

In Text A the first short sentence immediately grabs the reader's attention. It makes them ask the question: 'What happened in slow motion?' and want to read on to find the answer.

The rest of the paragraph provides the answer. The writer uses description to create an image of the crash as it actually happened.

It happened in slow motion. First, the squeal of the brakes as they fought and failed to slow the car down on the icy road; then, the tailspin as the road conditions sent the car into a crazy revolution towards the crash barrier; and finally the **sickening thud** on impact as **the car folded like an empty coke can**. Jake was aware of all of this but **powerless** to respond. It was as if his mind had frozen like an overworked computer and he simply stared in blank amazement as if he was watching but not involved. Then came the collision. Every window **shattered** on impact and **it rained glass**. The engine compartment was pushed backwards and, for the first time, Jake felt pain as the steering wheel was **pushed hard into his chest**. The airbag inflated but Jake still screamed as he felt two of his ribs crack under the strain. The pain was **excruciating** …

Activity

1 Re-read Text A closely and complete the following tasks. Keep a written record of your ideas.

a Look at the words that are underlined in Text A. How do these words help the reader experience the sights, sounds and feelings of the crash?

Think about:

- what the words tell you about the crash
- why the writer chose to use the underlined words.

Share your thoughts with another student.

b In pairs, discuss whether you think this is an effective opening. Give reasons why a reader may or may not want to read on.

Starting with characters

Some writers begin a story by introducing a major character. They hope to create a person who the reader will be interested in and want to know more about.

Read this opening to a story about a girl's feelings for a boy at the same school (Text B). In this case, the writer tells the story from the point of view of the girl, so she is telling the story. When writers use a character to tell the story, it is known as a first-person narrative. It allows the reader to know what that character is thinking and feeling throughout the story.

Ⓑ

The car glided to a halt outside the school and out stepped Sam. He leant back into the back seat, collected his canvas bag, threw it casually over his left shoulder and moved away easily, turning back once to wave to his mum, before striding out for the school gates. At six foot two inches tall, he towered above the Year 7 students walking alongside him, and his broad shoulders and narrow waist gave him an athletic look. His long black hair was sleek and brushed back, still slightly damp from his morning shower. He smiled and stood to one side to let me pass him as we both reached the school gates at the same time. His eyes were bright and alive with burning energy; the most stunning blue I had ever seen. I blushed and hoped he could not know what I was thinking. After all, he was Sam Clarke, or as the girls in my form often said: 'Tall, Clarke and handsome'.

2

a The writer of Text B presents a rather stereotyped picture of the school 'hunk'. List the details she uses to create a picture of Sam Clarke.

b What things do you learn about the narrator of this story from the opening paragraph?

c In pairs, discuss whether you think this is an effective opening. Give reasons why a reader might or might not want to read on.

As you have seen, writers try to catch the attention of their readers in the opening of a narrative. They create situations, events and characters and hope that the reader will want to find out more.

In the case of Text B, for instance, readers might want to know:

- whether Sam feels the same way about the girl as she does about him
- whether the other girls find out about her feelings
- why the writer has made him sound so perfect – will there be a twist in the tale?

Activity

3

Think about the opening of Text A. List three things that the writer might want to know after reading this first paragraph.

In looking at the openings to Texts A and B, you have seen how two writers have created action and character to attract the reader's attention. These are only two of the **devices** that writers can use at any point in a story to move it on and keep the reader's attention. They can also create setting, dialogue and contrast.

> **Key terms**
>
> **Device:** a writing method used for a particular purpose.

Setting

The setting is the place where the action happens. It can be a very important part of a narrative. Writers often use setting to create a particular mood or atmosphere. They need to choose their words carefully to make sure the setting matches what is happening in the story.

Texts C and D are two ways in which *Crash* could be continued. Both carry on the story by describing the scene immediately after the crash. The writer cannot decide which one to choose.

Activity

4 **a** Read Texts C and D. With a partner, make notes on:

- differences in the vocabulary chosen and the effects of these
- differences in the sentences used and the effects of these
- how the use of language affects the way the reader feels about the incident in each paragraph
- any further questions the texts raise in the reader's mind.

b Which continuation of the story do you think is more effective? Give your reasons.

C

After the noise of the impact the world went strangely quiet. There was smoke, the fire had not yet started, but no noise. There was only silence. Any observer would have been struck by the crash scene: a wheel trim here, a bumper bar there and the deep black marks the tyres had left on the road as the car had sped towards the barrier. But it was silent. Trapped inside the car, Jake made the first sound … a groan as the pain began to grow inside him.

D

From the sound and fury of the crash to deathly quiet in a split second. As if someone had flicked a switch, there was complete silence. The carriageway was strewn with wreckage, a wheel trim here, a bumper bar there, deep black tyre marks, like terrible scars, veered from the middle lane where the skid had started to the point of impact: where the car lay damaged and disfigured almost beyond recognition. But it was the silence that dominated.

Dialogue

Writers often develop the narrative through dialogue or conversation. The reader can learn a lot about a character through what they say and how they say it.

In the opening paragraph of Text B, the reader learns a little about the narrator's thoughts and feelings. The reader might suspect that the girl feels Sam is special by the way she describes how athletic he is and how his smile is reflected in his blue eyes. Sam has been described in detail but we know very little about him. Later in the story, the writer sets out to build on this by revealing more of the girl's inner thoughts and more about Sam (Text E).

5 Read Text E and answer the questions below. Work in pairs and keep a record of your answers. If you have a copy of the extract, you can highlight or underline parts of the story and make notes in the margin. Otherwise, make your notes on paper.

a Identify where the writer has revealed the narrator's thoughts and feelings.

b What do these thoughts and feelings add to your understanding of the narrator's character?

c What does the dialogue add to your understanding of:

- Sam
- the narrator
- the possibility of a relationship forming between them?

E

Our next meeting was at lunchtime in the dining hall. I was returning my tray having finished my lunch and was deep in conversation with Ellie. I did not even see him until after I had bumped into him, knocking him out of his stride and into the counter.

'Sorry,' I blurted out, as I turned to see what I had done.

'That's the second time today we've both been trying to get to the same place at the same time: first the school gate and now the dining hall. We get to all the best places!'

'Pardon?' I asked.

'Never mind. It's what passes for humour in my house. I was joking.'

He smiled and I smiled back.

'Oh well,' he concluded, 'I'll see you around but, please, if you want to talk to me, don't feel you need to attack me first.'

'Alright,' I replied and he was gone.

That afternoon, I found it hard to concentrate on Physics and Food Technology. My head was spinning. On the one hand, I was a clumsy oaf, who cannot even look where I am going. Then, when I have my big chance to talk to Sam, I manage three words, 'Sorry', 'Pardon' and 'Alright'. He must think I am an idiot. On the other hand, he did not react as most boys would and tell me to watch where I was going. And just what did he mean when he said, 'I'll see you around' and 'if you want to talk to me'. Did he want to talk to me? Or was it just a figure of speech?

Contrast

A good story does not have to be a long one. It does, however, need to be carefully structured and crafted. Remind yourself of the opening of Text A and the second paragraph that you selected for the writer. So far, the writer has created an image of the crash and of the scene immediately afterwards. Now read the next two paragraphs of the story (Text F), which present a contrast between the scene outside the car and the scene inside the car.

And now, suddenly, the motorway was like a war zone. There were people and machines everywhere. Three police cars blocked off the road and two policemen were in constant communication with base, keeping the road free of traffic and talking to the fire officers. There were two fire engines, parked on the hard shoulder. The firemen might have expected a fire, but that had been avoided. They paced the tarmac anxiously, frequently glancing at the car and the paramedics, waiting for the signal to use their cutting gear to get Jake out. Two ambulances were parked next to the car, their doors wide open and paramedics shuttled in and out to collect breathing apparatus, bandages and painkilling drugs. Through the dark night the flashing lights from the vehicles cast eerie shadows on the road.

Inside the car, it was a different story. Two paramedics were working quietly. Jake had been awake briefly when they arrived but in terrible pain. The first paramedic had sedated him and now he lay motionless, as if asleep. The second paramedic, a young woman, glanced at him while she worked. Even in the half-light, she could see how young he was with fine brown hair grown slightly long. The shirt she had cut open to get at his wounds was expensive and fashionable, very like one her husband wore. Turning to his injuries, she recognised how severe they were. Several of the cuts on his chest were seeping blood and her partner was struggling to stem the flow from his leg. Meanwhile, the doctor from the hospital leant over them in the cramped space, furiously massaging Jake's heart. This was not looking good.

6 Answer these questions to help you work out how the writer creates a contrast between the two paragraphs in Text F.

First paragraph:

a What simile is used in the opening sentence?

b What three different groups of people are at the scene of the accident?

c List five details which suggest this is a busy scene.

Second paragraph:

a What word in the first sentence suggests a contrast?

b How do the words 'quietly' and 'motionless' help to create this contrast?

c What is suggested by the final sentence?

Endings

A good story will have a good ending. It will usually leave the reader feeling that most, or all, of their questions about the story have been answered. If a question has kept the reader's attention throughout the story but never gets answered, the ending can be frustrating. Sometimes the writer deliberately introduces a new point in the ending to leave the reader asking a new question.

Now read the ending to *Crash* (Text G).

'Sarah, I think we're losing him,' the doctor said.

'His pulse is very weak,' her colleague added.

As if he was listening, Jake let out a heavy sigh and the heart monitor attached to his chest began to flatline, making its horrible piercing noise.

After just a few minutes the doctor turned to the paramedics. 'Are we all agreed?' he asked quietly, and they both nodded, without looking at him. They all hated this part.

'OK. Time of death 21.34,' the doctor announced, as he used two fingers to close Jake's eyes. He was still warm.

They all turned and walked to the ambulance, quiet, sombre, not one of them wanting to look back. The doctor headed for the policemen.

'We lost him, I'm afraid. He's all yours now. His wallet's on the passenger seat. Oh, and there's an 18th birthday present on the back seat. The card says, "To Paula. All my love, Jake".'

Activities

7

a This is the first time the writer uses dialogue in this story. Why do you think she decided to introduce this here?

b What new point is introduced at the very end of the story? What does this make you think of?

c Were you expecting the story to end in this way? Give reasons for your answer.

d Do you think this is a good ending? Give reasons for your answer.

8

a Sometimes writers have a twist in their tale. They lead the reader to expect a particular thing to happen and then present something unexpected. Remind yourself of Text B. With a partner, talk about:

- what you expect to happen
- what has led you to expect this.

b Still in pairs, list three different ideas for possible endings. Only one of them should be based on what you expect to happen. The others should give an unexpected twist to the story. Share your ideas with another pair. Choose the idea that you think would make the best ending. Explain why.

Check your learning

In this chapter you have learnt:

- How writers use the following to get and keep their readers attention:
  - openings
  - setting
  - dialogue
  - endings
- How to evaluate how effective these are.

Understanding arguments

Objectives

In this chapter you will:

learn how writers develop ideas using key points

understand how writers use fact and statistics to support their opinion and persuade their audience

examine the language writers use to influence their audience

consider why expert opinions are used in an argument.

An argument is a collection of linked points on a subject, in which a writer reveals their point of view. To follow the argument, the reader needs to be able to:

- understand and explain the key points
- work out how the writer is trying to influence the reader
- make judgements about the writer's viewpoint.

Writers use several techniques to help the reader follow the argument and persuade the reader to share their point of view. These include:

- clear key points, to make sure the reader focuses on the main points
- facts and statistics, to make their view seem correct
- emotive language, to influence the reader's feelings
- expert opinions, to back up their view
- their own viewpoint, to suggest interesting ideas and invite readers to agree.

Identifying key points

Text A is written for parents. It is about the eating habits of young children. The paragraphs of the article are numbered to make it easier for you to find the information you need to answer the questions on it. You will notice that some words are underlined and highlighted for use in activities later in the chapter.

To identify key points, you need to read the text closely. Sometimes the key point will appear in the first sentence of a paragraph and sometimes you will need to think about the whole paragraph to work out what it is.

So you think you know what your kids eat at school?

1 For breakfast, Jake ate a Real Fruit Winder and half a pack of Lunchables washed down with a Blackcurrant Blast-flavoured bottle of juice. Mum gave him a packet of crisps for breaktime, and at lunch he chose the turkey drummers with smiley faces followed by iced vanilla sponge and custard. 'I don't really like the broccoli or the salad stuff,' Jake says with a scowl. He is, though, looking forward to pizza for tea, followed by a Bat's Blood yoghurt with strawberry flavour sherbert.

2 At six years old, Jake is clearly fatter than his classmates. He does not yet know this, but as one of 80 million obese children in Europe, Jake is likely to live a shorter life than his parents. He is in danger of suffering from illnesses such as type-two diabetes. That is a lot for a boy to take in as he opens yet another packet of crisps.

3 Obesity in the UK has doubled in the last ten years, with about one in ten children affected. Health groups are warning of a crisis as overweight children reach adulthood. A less active lifestyle is partly to blame, but so is diet. According to the Government's National Diet and Nutrition Survey, 92 per cent of children eat more saturated fat than the recommended level for adults.

4 The food messages reaching children when parents are not present are increasingly worrying health workers. Cash-strapped schools are selling manufacturers a direct way to reach the primary-school 'marketplace'. They can, for a price, place their high-fat, high-sugar snacks directly into the children's hands, with no parents around to suggest they should be eating something healthier.

5 Over the past few months, a London based company has written to food manufacturers inviting them to buy in to a new marketing programme that directly targets school canteens. A brochure for the scheme explains that it is aimed at children as young as four, and includes

photographs of children enjoying sugary drinks and crisps. 'School canteens/dining halls are the ideal location for sampling produces,' the marketing kit boasts. 'Kids try the product and discuss with their friends,' and because this happens in the school canteen, it looks like the staff approve.

6 According to the Government's National Diet and Nutrition Survey, the average child in the UK drinks 15 glasses of sweet soft drinks every week. A recent study by the David Hide Asthma and Allergy Research Centre suggests that there is an indirect link between artificial colourings in drinks to hyperactivity in children.

7 At the International Obesity Task Force, Philip James claims if we don't act, 'the spread of childhood obesity is going to rip through Europe so fast – with Britain being in the worst category – that we will have hospitals full of diabetic children of 13, 14 years of age. The evidence is pretty clear that they will have major problems by the time they get into their thirties.'

Adapted from David Rowan, *The Observer*, 'Marketing food to children – investigation', 9 March 2003

Key terms

Obese: very overweight.

Type two diabetes: an inability to properly regulate blood sugar levels.

Hyperactivity: used to describe someone who is constantly active and excitable.

Activity

1 Using the paragraphs numbered 1–3 in Text A, answer the following questions:

a Using paragraph 1, what key point do you think the writer is making about Jake's diet?

b Using paragraph 2, list two possible consequences of Jake's unhealthy eating. Sum up the writer's key point in one sentence.

c In paragraph 3, the writer makes the key point in the opening sentence. What is it?

d What do the key points in paragraphs 1–3 suggest about the writer's views of children's eating habits?

e Read the rest of the article closely. For each paragraph, write one sentence that sums up its key point.

Use of facts and statistics

Writers often use **facts** and **statistics** to support their key points and add weight to their views. A fact is something that can be proved to be true – for example, the United Kingdom is in the northern hemisphere.

A statistic is a piece of information shown as a number – for example, the United Kingdom population reached 61.4 million in Mid-2008 having grown by 408,000 in the previous year.

Key terms

Fact: something that can be proved to be true.

Statistics: a piece of information shown as a number.

Activity

2 Using paragraph 3 of Text A, answer the following questions:

a Find two facts the writer gives about the increase in obesity in the last few years.

b One of the statistics has been highlighted for you in yellow. Find and write down one other statistic.

c What effect do you think these facts and statistics will have on the way a parent thinks about childhood obesity?

d Share your answers with another student. Did you have the same ideas?

Using emotive language

Using emotive language means using words to stir the feelings of the reader. Writers often use emotive language to build their argument and make it convincing. They might aim to make the reader feel – for example, sad, angry or amused.

Re-read paragraphs 4 and 5 of Text A in which the writer describes how fast-food firms and confectioners set out to target young children in school.

Activity

3

a In paragraph 4 of Text A, the writer's main concern is that schools are being used to market fast food to children. Using the underlined words in the paragraphs to help you, how do you think the writer wants parents to feel? Choose from the list below and explain the reasons for each choice you make.

- Worried
- Angry
- Excited
- Pleased
- Guilty
- Amused.

b In paragraph 5 of Text A, the writer describes the London-based advertising company brochure and quotes from it. Copy and complete the table below. Write the underlined words in the first column. In the second column, explain what the words suggest to you and what effect you think they are meant to have on the parents' feelings. The first one has been done for you.

Words/phrases	Expected amotional response
'directly targets school canteens'	The words 'directly target' emphasise that the company is doing this on purpose. The word 'targets' makes me think of something being fired at you and this suggests it's dangerous. I think the writer wants parents to feel angry and a little bit scared.
'as young as four'	
'the marketing kit boasts'	

Using expert opinion

A common technique used by writers to give weight to their arguments is to use quotes from experts and professionals. Sometimes they quote factual statements; at other times they report the opinions experts have given as if they are facts.

Read Text B, paragraph 6 of the article. The writer explains some of the consequences of poor eating habits. The annotations added below show you how expert opinion has been used.

The writer quotes a fact from a government report. It sounds alarming that children drink so many unhealthy drinks in a week

According to the Government's National Diet and Nutrition Survey, the average child in the UK drinks 15 glasses of sweet soft drinks every week. A recent study by the David Hide Asthma and Allergy Research Centre suggests that there is an indirect link between artificial colourings in drinks to hyperactivity and aggression in children.

This study is presented as important and alarming. However, the study only 'suggests' there could be a link between colourings and hyperactivity

Activity

4 In paragraph 7 of Text A, the writer quotes Philip James. The information that he is from the International Obesity Task Force adds weight to his opinions.

  a Explain the opinions expressed by Philip James.

  b Can you find examples of the use of emotive language in what Philip James says? List these.

  c What effect are these opinions likely to have on parents of young children?

  d Why do you think the writer ends with this paragraph?

  e Compare your answers with another student. Discuss any differences you have and make changes if necessary.

Making a judgement about the writer's opinion k!

In this chapter you have studied the techniques the writer uses to build his argument and to influence his reader. By now, you will realise that the writer is clearly worried about children's eating habits and the way they are targeted by food companies. He wants his readers to be persuaded by his argument. To help make sure of this, the writer selects the points he makes very carefully. For example, the following facts are not included in this article:

- Eating chocolate can be good for you.
- We no longer have the high levels of malnutrition that children suffered from in the 1940s.
- There are far fewer childhood deaths today than in the past.
- Why do you think these facts have not been included?

Activity

5 In a small group, talk about the points the writer makes. Do you think they are right? Imagine that the writer is in the classroom with you. What further questions would you ask him? What points of your own would you make to him? List these.

Check your learning

Use what you have learnt in this chapter to help you write a developed answer to the following two questions. Remember to use examples from Text A to support the points you make:

- How does the writer use facts, statistics and expert opinions to support his argument?
- How does the writer use words to influence and persuade the readers?

Responding to texts

Writers use a range of techniques to help the reader understand what they think and how they feel about the subject.

Fact and opinion

One way a writer may try to communicate her point of view is by using fact and **opinion** in her text.

Key terms

Opinion: a person's view about something, for example – Italy is the best place to visit on holiday – or science fiction films are better than romantic comedies.

Objectives

In this chapter you will:

work out how and why writers use facts and opinions

examine how writers use words to influence the reader

explore how a writer's point of view is revealed by the words they choose.

Activity

1

a Read the following sentences and decide whether each one is fact or opinion. Record your answers by making a list of facts and a list of opinions.

b Compare your answers with a partner. Discuss any sentences that you disagree on and alter your lists if necessary.

> Julius Caesar was a Roman Emperor.

> *Big Brother* is the worst programme on TV.

> Skiing is one of the most popular sports in Switzerland.

> Visiting an art museum is a good way to spend an afternoon.

> Hadrian's Wall passes through Northumberland and Cumbria.

> Fishing is cruel to fish.

To understand the writer's point of view, you need to be able to pick out the facts from the opinions and then work out how and why the writer is using them. In Text A, the facts have been highlighted in green and the opinions in blue.

Rome is the best city to visit for a summer holiday because it has the Vatican City, the Forum, lots of other places of interest and art museums, as well as hot, sunny weather and fantastic restaurants.

The writer is using facts to support her opinions to present a convincing argument. In this case she wants to persuade the reader that Rome is the best place for a holiday.

Activity

2

a The writer of Text A selected facts from the following list to support her point of view. Read the list below and choose five facts that you think could be used by someone who was unhappy with their visit there.

Facts about Rome

Attractions: Vatican City; the Forum; art museums.
Average summer temperature is 90°F.
12 euros for an ice cream, 17 euros for a pizza in tourist areas.
More than 7 million tourists visit Rome each year.
Street restaurants stay open after midnight.
The River Tiber runs through the city.
There are thieves and pickpockets in Rome.
Rome has a population of over 2.7 million.
Not all hotels have air conditioning.

b With a partner, discuss the facts you have chosen for your list. Have you noticed that:

- A person's opinion is shown by what they don't say (facts not used) as much as what they do say (facts used)?
- A fact can be used in a positive or negative way, for example: 'the weather in summer is hot and sunny'; 'the temperature in summer is an unbearable 90°F'?

Now read Text B from a magazine article reviewing a film, *The War Lords*.

The 'Bore' Lords

1 The long awaited screening of *The War Lords* turned out to be a massive disappointment on its Leicester Square premiere last night. A fantasy tale, set in the mythical land of Arkon, it sets a handsome warrior, Kryll, played by Ben Knight, against the ruthless Menwith, played by George Thornley. The plot sees Knight thrown into a dungeon and falsely accused of being a traitor by the king. After an unrealistic escape, which made even the 1970s *Star Trek* look action packed, Knight becomes a fugitive, trying to clear his name and save the kingdom before it is too late.

2 Stretching to two and a half hours, the film is at least 50 minutes too long and full of lengthy, dull conversations in which Knight pours out his heart to anyone who will listen. Being a medieval hero brings nothing but problems and more problems. At times, he seems more like a worrier than a warrior. Long before the end it is clear that comedy actor, Ben Knight, should stick to delivering funny lines rather than saving the universe.

Activity

3

a Copy the words and phrases that have been highlighted in the first paragraph of Text C. For each one, say whether you think it is a fact or an opinion.

b For each opinion, say what it tells you about the writer's point of view.

c With a partner, read through paragraph 2 of Text B and pick out the phrases or words that are opinion.

d What is the writer's view of this film? Use one of the opinions you have chosen from the text to back up your idea.

Using words to influence the reader 🄺

Writers also choose words to create a certain impression. Look at the following newspaper headlines written about the same football match (Text C). They show the way in which two different spectators have written about the same game to reveal their different views.

(D) **DULL CITY LACK ADVENTURE IN LOCAL DERBY**

This suggests that City made no attempt to play in an entertaining, attacking way.

BRAVE CITY DEFEND VALIANTLY IN LOCAL DERBY

This suggests that City were under a lot of pressure, but the defence played well.

The two writers have used the same type of sentence, but have used words to give the reader two completely different impressions of the same match.

Activity

4 Read the following headlines in the table below. The underlined words have been chosen to create a particular impression. Copy the headlines, replacing the underlined words with words that create a different impression. The first one has been done for you.

COMPUTER GAMES IMPROVE TEENAGERS' MINDS	COMPUTER GAMES DAMAGE TEENAGERS' MINDS
CHILDREN'S TV CRITICISED IN NEW REPORT	
POLITICIAN PRAISES NEW EXAMS AS THE WAY FORWARD	
COUNCIL CLAIMS HEALTHY EATING IMPROVES STUDENTS' WORK	
VILLAGERS ANGRY ABOUT PLANNED BY-PASS	

Recognising the writer's viewpoint

Writers choose their words carefully to reflect their views on a subject. As a reader, you need to think carefully about the words a writer chooses and work out what is being suggested by them.

Text E is part of an article on the Trafford Centre, which is a large shopping complex in Manchester. The first paragraph has been annotated to show the thoughts and questions of a reader who is thinking carefully. Read the text and the annotations before moving on to Activity 5.

The Trafford Centre

The Trafford Centre is huge. As you approach it from the motorway, you cannot help but notice its two blue glass domes that dominate the skyline. It stands like some great cathedral waiting to welcome its congregation. On a busy day, avoiding the traffic can be a nightmare, but once you have left your car in one of its many spacious car parks, you are free to sample the delights of shopping, Manchester style.

'dominates' suggests it rules ... is the writer suggesting that it's very impressive or that it stands out in a bad way?

This makes it sound as though people treat shopping as though it was a religion. Does the writer think that's a good or a bad thing?

Well, that's definitely a bad thing!

Is the writer being serious or sarcastic?

The Trafford Centre is so popular that crowds descend on its marbled hallways like bees to a honey pot. Coaches from Liverpool, Cumbria and Wales rest their weary engines in its car parks, having unloaded thousands of shoppers to trudge up and down the malls in a crowd scene that looks like the neighbouring Old Trafford Football Ground on a match day. There, they marvel at how much the Trafford Centre's Debenhams is so much like the same store in their own town and at how you can always rely on McDonald's.

As they leave, they display their shopping to make sure that others can see the expensive designer carrier bags which contain their reward for braving the crowds. Then it's into their cars, coaches and buses and off home to count the cost of their wonderful day out. The Trafford Centre: a place where Debenhams meets Disney to create shopping heaven!

Activity

5

a With a partner, discuss the remaining highlighted words in paragraphs 2 and 3 of Text E and what you think the writing is suggesting by their use.

b Which of the following statements do you think best reflects the writer's attitude to the Trafford Centre? You can choose more than one. For each one you choose, find one or two pieces of evidence in the text to support your choice.

> The writer thinks it's a fantastic place to go to.

> The writer would rather go to a football match.

> The writer seems to really dislike the Trafford Centre.

> The writer thinks it is like heaven.

> The writer thinks shopping is as good as religion.

> The writer recognises that lots of people like to go there.

> The writer mocks the people who go there to shop.

> The writer thinks it offers nothing new.

c Compare your choices with another student. Discuss any differences you have.

Writing about viewpoint

Students who read carefully and have good ideas about what they are reading sometimes find it difficult to put those ideas into writing. The following student learnt a useful way of how to do this in Year 9. Read the opening of his answer to the question: What do you learn about the writer's attitude to the Trafford Centre? The annotations show you how he has constructed his answer.

❶ Makes a statement about the writer's use of language

❷ Uses supporting evidence from the text

(F)

The writer uses negative language to describe the Trafford Centre. ❶ For example, he says that the traffic is a 'nightmare'. ❷ This suggests that getting to and from the centre can be very difficult and unpleasant. ❸

❸ Comments on evidence

Activity

6 Copy down one of the statements from Activity 5b with which you agreed. Write a sentence using two pieces of supporting evidence. Comment on the evidence you have given.

The student who wrote Text F wasn't happy with his answer. He had more things to say and he knew he could do better. He decided to have another go and try to put more detailed comments into his writing, which would show that he had thought carefully when reading the text. Text G is his second attempt. The annotations show you how he developed his answer.

❶ Makes a statement about the writer's use of language

❸ Comments on evidence

❹ Develops comment on evidence

❻ Comments on evidence

(G)

The writer seems to have a negative view of the Trafford Centre. ❶ He says that 'On a busy day, avoiding the traffic can be a nightmare'. ❷ Using the word 'nightmare' suggests this is an unpleasant experience. ❸ The use of the word 'avoiding' suggests that it is not just unpleasant for those going to the centre, but might have an impact on other people on the roads too. ❹ This view is backed up later in the article when the writer states that the shoppers 'marvel at how much the Debenhams is so much like the same store in their own town'. ❺ This implies that the place is dull and the same as any shopping centre anywhere. ❻ It's also said in a sarcastic way, as though the writer is mocking the shoppers because they go all there even though they have the same shops at home. ❼

❷ Uses supporting evidence from the text

❺ Introduces more evidence from a different part of the text

❼ Gives own interpretation of the evidence

a Look back at what you wrote for Activity 6. Use the seven points given with Text F to help you develop your writing. Aim to write 100–150 words and to show that you are a thinking reader.

b Swap your writing with another student's. Annotate it using the student's developed response on page 55 to help you.

Check your learning

Use what you have learnt in this chapter to help you examine the writer's point of view in Text G.

a Make notes on:

- facts used by the writer
- opinions used by the writer
- words used to influence the reader
- the writer's viewpoint.

b Use your notes to help you write a developed answer to the question: What do you learn about the writer's attitude to the Barton Square extension?

New Trafford Centre wing

THE wraps have come off the Trafford Centre's dazzling £90m Barton Square extension.

The Italian-style piazza comes complete with a 173ft-tall bell tower and features a host of new and exciting shops selling furniture and domestic goods.

The first phase of the development – which includes Habitat, Next Home, Dwell and British Home Stores – has already received 50,000 satisfied visitors after it opened just in time for Easter.

Barton Square's second phase is set to include the opening of the world's largest Marks & Spencer Home store in April, followed by further store openings such as Home Sense and Natuzzi in May.

Local people will benefit from the creation of up to 500 new jobs, thanks to the 200,000sq ft building.

Trafford Centre director of operations, Gordon McKinnon, said: 'We are thrilled that Barton Square has attracted so many visitors in its first week of trading, and we hope that this trend continues as more new stores open over the coming months.'

Adapted from Dean Kirby, *Manchester Evening News*, 26 March 2008

Objectives

In this chapter you will:

develop your ideas about texts

explore the author's viewpoint

learn how to explain your ideas using evidence.

Following clues

Some questions you might ask when reading a text are:

● What is it about?

● What is the writer thinking?

● How is the writer feeling?

● What does the writer want me to think and feel?

You cannot know for certain, unless you ask the writer, but you can use evidence and clues in the text to help you get some idea of the answers. In the following autobiographical text, the writer is recalling an important event that happened when he was younger. Read the first paragraph closely.

A I waved goodbye for the final time with a heavy heart and closed the garden gate. It was a raw night. The moon was covered and a thin glimmer from the street lamps lit my way. I turned up my collar, and thrust my hands deep into my pockets and trudged along the footpath towards home. It was midnight and I had promised I would be back an hour earlier. There would be hell to pay, I knew that, but time spent with Laura was precious now. Soon she would be off to London and I would be left, 200 miles away, in Carrington. I began the long slow plod to Campbell Avenue and the reception party that awaited me.

Activity

1 Use evidence and clues in the text to help you answer these questions.

a What have you learnt about the writer's situation?

b What have you learnt about the writer's feelings about Laura?

c What do you think the writer is feeling as he walks home? Now read Text B.

B I turned off the main road and headed for the path alongside the golf course. This was not my preferred route as it could be muddy and, since it was unlit, I would not be able to see clearly where I was walking. Still, it was better than taking the longer route. That would take even more time and further anger my parents, not a good idea. Muddy trainers were the least of my worries. The first suggestion that I was not alone came after I had walked about 30 yards from the security of the road and the streetlights. A twig snapped. I peered into the blackness. Nothing. I told myself I had imagined the sound and returned to my journey, shivering slightly.

2 Answer these questions:

- What different clues does the writer give to suggest to the reader that there may be danger ahead?
- How does the writer want the reader to feel at the end of this paragraph?

3 Now think about both paragraphs. For each piece of evidence below (a–c), complete the sentence by explaining what you think it shows or suggests. Remember it is up to you how you interpret the evidence. There is no right or wrong answer.

Here is an example before you start:

'I told myself I had imagined the sound and returned to my journey, shivering slightly'.
This final line of the extract reinforces the idea that although the boy is trying to convince himself that there is nothing wrong, he might be in danger or that he is not alone.

a 'Soon she would be off to London and he would be left' suggests that …

b The boy 'trudged along the footpath towards his home'. This makes me think the writer must be feeling …

c When the writer refers to dirty trainers as 'the least of his worries', this gives the reader the idea that …

Clues and culture

Writers often give readers clues about their thoughts, feelings and what is going to happen. Sometimes, though, we need extra information to help us to fully understand and interpret a text. Texts often reflect the cultural background of the writer. An understanding of this background can help you to better understand the text and the writer's point of view.

You are going to read some details about the writer Tatamkhulu Afrika, before reading a poem he wrote. This will help you to understand what he was thinking and how he was feeling when he wrote the poem.

Biography

Tatamkhulu Afrika (1920–2002) grew up happily in South Africa in Cape Town's District 6, a mixed-race inner-city community.

In the 1960s, the government declared District 6 a 'whites-only' area as part of its policy of separating races, known as apartheid. The South African government began to classify every citizen by colour – white, black and coloured. Over several years, the entire area was cleared. Most of it has never been built on.

The poem was written just after the official end of apartheid. It was a time of hope – Nelson Mandela had recently been released from prison, and was about to lead the new government of South Africa.

Tatamkhulu Afrika was raised in Cape Town, South Africa, as a white South African. Here are some facts about his life:

- When he was a teenager, he found out that he was actually Egyptian-born – with an Arab father and a Turkish mother.
- Afrika turned down the chance to be classed as white, deciding instead to become a Muslim and be classified as coloured.
- He was arrested in 1987 for terrorism and banned from writing or speaking in public for five years.
- He changed his name to Tatamkhulu Afrika – which had previously been his terrorist code name. This allowed him to carry on writing, despite the ban.

Activities

4 a Read the biography information of Tatamkhula Afrika.

b Now read the following sentences about him and decide whether they are true or false:

- Tatamkhulu Afrika liked living in District 6.
- Apartheid was a way of encouraging different races to mix together.
- The poem was written when the policy of apartheid had ended.
- Afrika wanted to be known as white, but was classified as coloured.
- Afrika changed his name to allow him to continue writing and speaking in public.

c When you have completed Activity 4b, compare your answers with a partner and discuss any differences you may have.

5 Now read Afrika's poem 'Nothing's Changed' (Text C) and make notes to the questions next to it.

a The first verse helps the reader to picture the scene. What kind of scene is it?

b How do the words 'click', 'bearded seeds' and 'crunch' add to your understanding of the scene?

c What does verse 2 tell you about the poet's feelings? Which words help you to understand these feelings?

d What do the words 'Brash with glass', 'flaring like a flag' and 'squats' tell you about the poet's feelings about the new restaurant?

e What does the poet mean by the words: 'we know where we belong'?

f What kind of restaurant does the poet describe? How do you know?

g Why does the poet include the verse about the kind of café that working men would use?

h What does the last verse show you about the effect on the poet of his visit to District 6?

ⓒ Nothing's Changed

Small hard round stones click
under my heels
seeding grasses thrust
bearded seeds
into trouser cuffs, cans,
trodden on, crunch
in tall, purple-flowering,
amiable weeds.

District Six.
No board says it is:
but my feet know,
and my hands,
And the skin about my bones,
and the soft labouring of my lungs,
and the hot, white, inwards
turning
anger of my eyes.

Brash with glass,
name flaring like a flag,
it squats
in the grass and weeds,
incipient Port Jackson trees:
new, up-market, haute cuisine,
guard at the gatepost,
whites only inn.

No sign says it is:
but we know where we belong.

I press my nose
to the clear panes, know
before I see them, there will be
crushed ice white glass,
linen falls,
the single rose.

Down the road
working man's café sells
bunny chows.
Take it with you, eat
it at a plastic table's top,
wipe your fingers on your jeans,
spit a little on the floor:
it's in the bone

I back from the glass,
boy again,
leaving small mean O
of small, mean mouth.
Hands burn
for a stone, a bomb,
to shiver down the glass.
Nothing's changed.

Tatamkhulu Afrika, 'Nothing's Changed'

Here are some explanations of the language in Text C that you may not be familiar with, they have been highlighted in red in the text:

Trouser cuffs: turn ups.

Brash: loud and showy.

Flaring: shining brightly.

Incipient Port Jackson trees: newly planted trees imported from Australia. For example, trees not native to Africa.

Up-market, haute cuisine: expensive, stylish way of cooking and presenting food.

Crushed ice white glass: expensive crystal glass.

Linen falls: fancy white tablecloths and napkins.

Bunny chows: bread stuffed with pilchards or similar.

Reading between the lines

When you interpret a text you have to work out the thoughts and feelings of the writer. You develop your own ideas about the text based on what the writer says and on the ideas you get from the writer's words.

Understanding the writer's perspective

As you have learned in Text C, a writer's perspective is their point of view. Writers develop ideas according to their own opinions and the way they view the world. Read the following texts in which writers reveal their views about their experiences as travellers.

Activity

6 Write six to eight lines to explain how you think Tatamkhulu Afrika might have felt about the way of life in South Africa after his visit to District 6. Use evidence from the text to support what you say. Include your ideas on:

● his impressions of how it is being developed
● his opinion of the restaurant
● what he says about what working men eat and the way they eat it
● what he may have felt after his visit.

Activity

7

a With a partner, read the passage about Sorrento (Text D) and text mark any words and phrases that suggest that the writer really likes the place. Think about:

- the writer's opening comments
- opinions she expresses
- details or features of the town and surrounding area she describes and their effect on the reader
- the words the writer uses to describe both Sorrento and her thoughts and feelings about it.

D Sorrento, Italy

Sorrento is quite simply the jewel in Italy's crown. I fell in love with it the first time I saw it! On my first visit, I arrived at night. I could see only the twinkling lights of the neighbouring villages and dark indistinct shapes covered by the blackness of the night. Next morning, when I threw back the shutters to my bedroom window, there, stretched out before me, was the Bay of Naples and clinging to the cliff face above it was the town itself.

I think the colours were the first things I noticed. The orange terracotta roof tiles, the grey green leaves of the thousands of olive trees covering the hillsides, and, dominating the whole scene was the bright blue of the sea. It was so blue that it took my breath away. On the far side of the bay stood Mount Vesuvius, the legendary volcano that swamped Pompeii 2,000 years ago. On that day it looked harmless, as if it was made of polystyrene. The sky was so clear that it looked as if one could reach out and touch the slopes …

b Copy and complete the table below, the first one has been done for you.

Feature for comparison	Example	Effect on reader
Opening lines	'Sorrento is quite simply the jewel in Italy's crown. I fell in love with it the first time I saw it'	Suggests that this is going to be a positive piece about a well-loved, favourite town.
Opinions the writer gives about Sorrento		
Details or features of the town and surrounding area		
Words used to describe Sorrento and the writer's opinion of it		

Writing your own interpretation

In Activity 7 you found features of the text that showed the writer's thoughts and feelings. Now you are going to look at this interpretation (Text E) by a student in response to the following question: How does the author of 'Sorrento, Italy' reveal his opinions of the town?

E

The writer begins in a very positive way. When she says 'I fell in love with it the first time I saw it' it makes me think this is going to be filled with happy memories of Sorrento. This is confirmed when she begins to write in detail. She includes attractive features such as 'orange terracotta roof tiles, the grey green leaves of the thousands of olive trees' and 'the bright blue of the sea'. He seems delighted by the beautiful colours of the landscape and the detail in which she writes possibly suggests that she is also fascinated by it. Perhaps she has not seen anything with such beauty before. I wondered why she went on to mention the history of Mount Vesuvius, which he describes as having 'swamped Pompeii 2,000 years ago'.

Useful phrase for considering effect on the reader

Includes brief details from the text to develop point of view

Useful words to introduce interpretation

Shows how ideas are to be developed later in the text

The highlighted text and notes show how the student has:

- expressed his thoughts and opinions
- used evidence from the text to support his ideas.

Now you are going to prepare to write your own interpretation of the writer's viewpoint of Sousse in Tunisia.

Activity

8

a With a partner, read the passage (Text F) about Sousse and text mark any words and phrases that suggest that the writer does not like the place. Think about:

- the writer's opening comments
- opinions he expresses

- details or features of the town and surrounding area he describes and their effect on the reader
- the words the writer uses to describe both Sousse and thoughts and feelings about it.

F

Sousse, Tunisia

The best thing about visiting Sousse was leaving it. I had not prepared myself for anything so different to my usual European trips, and pretty soon I was regretting my decision to venture further afield to experience Africa.

My first impression, apart from the searing heat, was the lack of vegetation and colour. Everything was desert like: sand, sand and more sand. It was everywhere. On the journey from the airport, I had hoped to appreciate the scenery, but there was nothing to enjoy. The town was old and rundown. We passed the market and various random shops. No signs marked out their owner's names or what they sold. To a European like me, it seemed haphazard and disorganised.

I told myself I would feel better after a meal and made my way down to the hotel restaurant. There was no air conditioning. Within two minutes,

the effect of my shower had worn off and I was dripping once more. The food arrived with a swarm of flies drawn by the spices and the prospect of a meal … my meal.

I sat back. The television advertisement played in my mind: 'In your dreams, you have been to Tunisia.' This was not the dream I had hoped for. This was a nightmare …

b Copy and complete the table below, the first one has been done for you.

Features	Example	Effect on reader
Opening lines	'The best thing about visiting Sousse was leaving it'	Makes it clear that the writer is about to describe something he did not enjoy
Opinions the writer gives about Sousse		
Details or features of the town and surrounding areas		
Words used to describe Sousse and the writer's opinion of it		

Check your learning

Look again at the description of Sousse (Text F) and write one paragraph in response to the following questions: How does the writer reveal his feelings about Sousse or the events he describes? What is the effect of this description on the reader?

In your answer you should:

- show how the opening lines relate to the rest of the text
- refer briefly to details from the text
- explain the effect on you of particular words and phrases
- use appropriate vocabulary to make your points and to introduce your interpretation.

10

Objectives

In this chapter you will:

learn how to make comparisons between texts

find similarities and differences between texts

plan and write a comparison.

Key terms

Criteria: things on which we base our judgements.

Comparing texts

When we compare two or more things, we are trying to see what similarities and differences there are between them. Often, this leads to making a judgement about whether one is better than another.

Making a comparison

Someone who wants to buy a new mobile phone might look at features of different phones before deciding which one to buy. These features might include:

- camera
- brand
- colour
- screen.

They could use these features as the **criteria** to help them decide which phone to buy. They do not need to consider every feature a phone has – just the ones that are most important to them in making a decision.

Activities

1   What other features or criteria might you use when buying a new mobile phone? Copy out the list and add your new criteria, then place them in order of importance to you.

2   **a**   Read Texts A and B on page 64, which are both advertisements for mobile phones. Copy the table below and complete the first column using the features on your list.

   b   Complete the second and third columns by identifying those features in both phones.

   c   Complete the final two columns by noting any important similarities or differences between them.

3   Use your completed table to help you decide which phone you would buy. Explain the reasons for your choice.

Feature	TC DL750 Epic Silver	Elite E100 Black	Similiarities	Differences
Camera	5 megapixels autofocus	3.2 megapixels autofocus	Autofocus	Phone A is bigger

A

TC DL750 Epic Silver

The TC DL750 Epic Silver is the new and exciting touch screen phone from DL. Most of its front face contains a 3 inch screen, which makes it great for reviewing pictures, watching videos and internet browsing. It's very sleek and will draw attention for all of the right reasons.

It has a new 3D touch user interface named V-Class, which is simply stunning. The touch screen is amazingly sensitive. Initial reports claim that this is the most impressive touch screen phone since the iPhone was launched.

The phone has a 5 megapixel camera with the highly rated Manz lens and autofocus. It can record DVD quality video and it has DivX playback too. There's 8GB of internal memory, which can be expanded up to 24GB by adding a 16GB micro SD memory card.

Get one now for only £150.

B

Elite E100 Black

The Elite E100 is a high-end, high-quality E-series smartphone with a slide out QWERTY keyboard. Considering this, it's relatively slim and compact, just 14.4mm thick. The steel-plated back of the phone oozes quality and style and the slide out keyboard is in a different class as it is framed with chrome, very solid and is a joy to use.

The 2.4 inch screen is among the best on the market and is even readable in direct sunlight. There are a whole host of email clients supported. With 3G, HSDPA and Wi-Fi, this is a very handy device to have outside of the office and makes the Elite E100 even better than the class-leading E71 when it comes to messaging and organisation. It also has GPS and a 4GB memory card is included. The camera has a 3.2 megapixel autofocus camera with dual LED flash.

£140 *offers apply.

The language of comparison

Text C is part of a comparison of the two phones. The features of the comparison are highlighted and annotated for you.

Ⓒ These two phones have a lot to offer. They are similar in that they both have cameras with autofocus. However, the camera on the TC has 5 megapixels while the Elite has only 3.2.

When it comes to functionality, the TC can record DVD quality video and it has DivX playback too. So, if you are looking for something to use for viewing media and browsing the Internet, the TC would be worth a look. On the other hand, the Elite is good for messaging and organising.

Points out features of both phones.

Uses language of comparison to link similarities and point out the differences between the phones.

Offers opinion while recognising that the buyer will choose the phone which best suits his or her needs.

The writer has used particular words such as 'however' to make his comparisons. Other words you can use to point out similarities and differences between texts are listed below:

Words or phrases used to point out similarities:	Words or phrases used to point out differences:
• similarly • both • in the same way • also • like.	• while • but • on the other hand • whereas • instead.

Activity

4
a Use the information in the table you created for Activity 2 to write your own article for teenagers in which you compare the two phones and offer your opinion on each one.

b When you have finished, swap your writing with another student's. Highlight:
- the details you have included about the phones
- the words used to make comparisons
- the opinions given.

Comparing poems

Once you understand how to compare two things, you can transfer those skills to other texts. You are now going to compare two poems.

When we read poems, we normally use four criteria to help us make an informed judgement on them. These are:
- what the poem is about – its **content**
- how the poet uses words to affect the reader
- how the poem is structured and presented
- how we respond to the poem.

Read Text D 'The Thickness of Ice' by Liz Loxley on page 66. In this poem, Liz Loxley describes a relationship. By comparing it to skating on ice, she shows the stages of the relationship. The brackets help the reader to understand the thoughts of one of the people involved.

Key terms

Content: what the text is about – the subject of the text.

The Thickness of Ice

At first we'll meet as friends
(Though secretly I'll be hoping
we'll become much more
and hoping that you're hoping that too.)

At first we'll be like skaters
testing the thickness of ice
(with each meeting
we'll skate nearer the centre of the lake.)

Later we will become less anxious to impress
less eager than the skater going for gold.
(The triple jumps and spins
will become an old routine,
we will become content with simple movements.)

Later we will not notice the steady thaw,
the creeping cracks will be ignored.
(And one day when the ice gives way
we will scramble to save ourselves
and not each other.)

Last of all we'll meet as acquaintances
(though secretly we'll be enemies,
hurt by missing out on a medal,
jealous of new partners).

Last of all we'll be like children
Having learnt the thinness of ice,
(though secretly, perhaps, we may be hoping,
to break the ice between us
and meet again as friends).

Liz Loxley, 'The Thickness of Ice'

Activity

5

With a partner, discuss and make notes in answer to these questions:

a Think about the opening phrase of each stanza. What, according to the speaker, are the three stages of the relationship?

b Do you think the poet is writing about one particular relationship, or relationships in general? Give reasons for your answer.

c Which of the following might describe the poet's point of view? You can choose more than one. Explain your choice(s) using evidence from the poem.

- She is bitter about a failed relationship.
- She thinks that most relationships fail in the end.
- She is convinced love will lasts forever.
- She thinks you need to work hard to make a relationship work.
- She is sad that she has lost a friend.

d The poet compares the people to skaters. What does each of the following lines add to your understanding of how the relationship develops?

- 'testing the thickness of ice'
- 'less eager than the skater going for gold.'
- 'the creeping cracks will be ignored.'

e Find three more examples of words and phrases that the poet uses to show the relationship. Explain how these phrases help your understanding of it.

f How is the poem structured and presented? Think about:

- the order of events
- similarities/differences in the stanzas form and the reasons for these
- the use of punctuation.

g Do you agree with the view on relationships given in this poem? Give reasons for your answer.

h Is the poem effective? Give reasons for your answer.

Activity

6 Copy the following table, which will help to make your comparison of two poems easier. Use your notes on Activity 5 above to help you complete the second column. Include quotations to support your points. (Keep your table for later activities.)

Criteria	The Thickness of Ice (Text D)	I never said I loved you, John (Text E)	Similiarities	Differences
Content				
Use of language				
Structure and presentation				
Your personal response				

Now read Text E, a poem by Christina Rossetti. The poet writes about a man, John, and his feelings for a woman who does not feel the same way about him.

(E)

I never said I loved you, John

I never said I loved you, John:
Why will you tease me day by day,
And wax a weariness to think upon
With always 'do' and 'pray'?

You know I never loved you, John;
No fault of mine made me your toast:
Why will you haunt me with a face as wan
As shows an hour-old ghost?

I dare say Meg or Moll would take
Pity upon you, if you'd ask:
And pray don't remain single for my sake
Who can't perform the task.

I have no heart? Perhaps I have not;
But then you're mad to take offence
That don't give you what I have not got:
Use your common sense.

Let bygones be bygones:
Don't call me false, who owed not to be true:
I'd rather answer 'No' to fifty Johns
Than answer 'Yes' to you.

Let's mar our pleasant days no more,
Song-birds of passage, days of youth:
Catch at today, forget the days before:
I'll wink at your untruth.

Let us strike hands as hearty friends;
No more, no less; and friendship's good:
Only don't keep in view ulterior ends, and
points not understood

In open treaty. Rise above
Quibbles and shuffling off and on:
Here's friendship for you if you like; but love –
No, thank you, John.

Christina Rossetti, 'I never said I loved you, John'

7   With a partner, discuss and make notes in answer to these questions:

a   The speaker appears to be answering points made by John about their relationship. What different things do you think John has said to her? How does she reply to him?

b   Find three examples which suggest, through the use of words, that this poem is part of a conversation.

c   This poem was first published in 1862. Can you find examples of the way language is used that is different to today? Write the examples down and explain the difference.

d   How is repetition used for effect in the following stanza? Find other examples of the use of repetition in the poem.

> Let's mar our pleasant days no more,
> Song-birds of passage, days of youth:
> Catch at today, forget the days before:
> I'll wink at your untruth.

e   How is the poem structured and presented? Think about:
  ● how the conversation develops
  ● similarities/differences in the stanza form and the reasons for these
  ● the use of rhyme and punctuation.

f   Although there are clues to what John has said, we are only given the woman's side of the conversation. How does this affect your response to the poem?

g   How do you think the poet feels about this relationship? (Note: this question is about the poet, not the speaker.) Explain why you think this.

h   Is the poem effective? Give reasons for your opinion.

8   **a**   Use your answers to Activity 7 to help you complete the third column in the table copied from Activity 6. Remember to include quotations to support your points.

b   With a partner, discuss similarities and differences between the two poems. Note these in the final two columns.

Writing the response

You are almost ready to use what you have learnt in this chapter and write a comparison of these two poems. However, first, you need to think about how to structure your comparison. You could use the following structure:

● Write your title: A comparison of 'The Thickness of Ice' by Liz Loxley and 'I never said I loved you, John' by Christina Rossetti.

● Start with a short paragraph in which you point out that both poems are about relationships, but that they give us different views on these.

● Write about the content of both poems, pointing out similarities and differences. Use the first row of your table from Activity 6 to help you.

- Write about the use of language in both poems, pointing out similarities and differences. Use the second row of your table to help you.
- Write about the structure and presentation in both poems, pointing our similarities and differences. Use the third row of your table to help you.
- Write about your personal response to each poem and, if you have a preference, say what it is and the reasons for it. Use the final row of your table to help you.

Remember to:

- include quotations to support the points you make
- use words that will help you make comparisons for example 'This is similar to …'

Activity

a Use what you have learnt in this chapter to help you write a comparison of the two poems *The Thickness of Ice* (Text D) and *I never said I loved you, John* (Text E). Follow the structure given above. Write five paragraphs.

b When you have finished writing, read through what you have written to make sure it makes clear sense.

Review and reflect

Throughout this chapter you have learnt to make comparisons between different kinds of text. A good way of remembering how to do this is to think of the word ELM.

E: establish the criteria to be used for comparison.

L: locate the information or evidence for each of the items you are comparing.

M: make a judgement about the items based on the criteria.

Stretch yourself

Choose two poems that you are studying from your AQA Anthology. Make a table like the one you made in Activity 6 and record your ideas about each poem.

Check your learning

Look back through this chapter and remind yourself of the different areas of study.

Then check you have:

- compared content, use of language, structure and presentation
- given your personal response
- used quotations to support the points you make.

11

Making your reading skills count in the exam

About the exam

In your study of the past ten chapters, you have been developing your skills in reading. These skills will help you do well in the exam.

There is one exam paper in GCSE English and GCSE English Language. Its focus is:

● understanding and producing non-fiction texts.

The paper is divided into two sections:

● **Section A**: Reading (one hour) 20% of your final marks.
● **Section B**: Writing (one hour) 20% of your final marks.

In the Reading section, you will be asked to read four non-fiction items and answer six questions. There will be at least one question on each item. The final question will ask you to compare two items of your choice. You will be asked to focus on a particular feature such as presentational features or use of language.

The non-fiction items are likely to be taken from magazines, newspapers, books, leaflets, advertisements and/or web pages. You will be able to make notes or highlight key points on these.

You will be given an answer booklet containing the questions and space for your answers.

What you need to know

You have one hour in which to show the examiner the reading skills summarised in the Assessment Objectives. These are printed below. The annotations explain what you have to do.

Assessment Objectives

Work out the meaning of the words and pictures and what they suggest

Select detail in order to answer the question

Read and understand texts, selecting material appropriate to purpose, collating from different sources and making comparisons and cross references as appropriate.

Select and use material from two different texts

Point out similarities and differences between texts

Write about the words used, the order in which the words are placed, the way the text is organised, and the use of presentational features

Refer to the text to support your points

Give your opinion

Focus on the techniques

Explain and evaluate how writers use linguistic, grammatical, structural and presentational features to achieve effects and influence the reader, supporting comments with detailed textual references.

Explain how the writer/designer is trying to affect the reader

Sample questions

The questions in the exam are based on the Assessment Objectives. Here are six sample exam questions. The marks awarded for each answer are given. Match the highlighted letters at the side of each question to the grid at the bottom of the page to find out what skills you are being tested on.

Read Item 1, *True Story,* and answer the question below.

1   List **four** things that you **should** do if you get caught in a rip without a board or inflatable. (*4 marks*)

   A B

Now read Item 2, *Walt Disney World For Teens,* and answer the question below.

2   List **six** different reasons why, according to this web page, teenagers might enjoy Walt Disney World. (*6 marks*)

   A B

3   Choose **three** examples of the way language is used for effect in this web page. Write each example down and explain how each example is being used for effect. (*6 marks*)

   A B E

Now read Item 3, *Bring Out Your Inner Ape!,* and answer the question below.

4   How has the designer of this leaflet organised the information and the pictures to have an impact on the reader? (*8 marks*)

   A B F G

Now read Item 4, *The Boys Are Back In Town,* and answer the question below.

5   How does the writer use language to interest and inform the reader? (*8 marks*)

   A B E G

Now look at all four items and answer the question below.

6   Choose **two** of these items which use presentational devices. Compare the ways presentational devices are used in them in order to interest the reader. (*8 marks*)

   A B C D E G

Skills being tested
A Read and understand texts
B Select material appropriate to purpose
C Collate material from different sources
D Make comparisons and cross-reference as appropriate
E Explain and evaluate how writers use linguistic and grammatical features to achieve effects and influence the reader
F Explain and evaluate how writers/designers use structural and presentational features to achieve
G Support comments with detailed textual references

1 The texts referred to in these sample questions are printed on the following pages. With a partner, read them closely. Make notes on the answers you would give to each question.

The items

Item 1

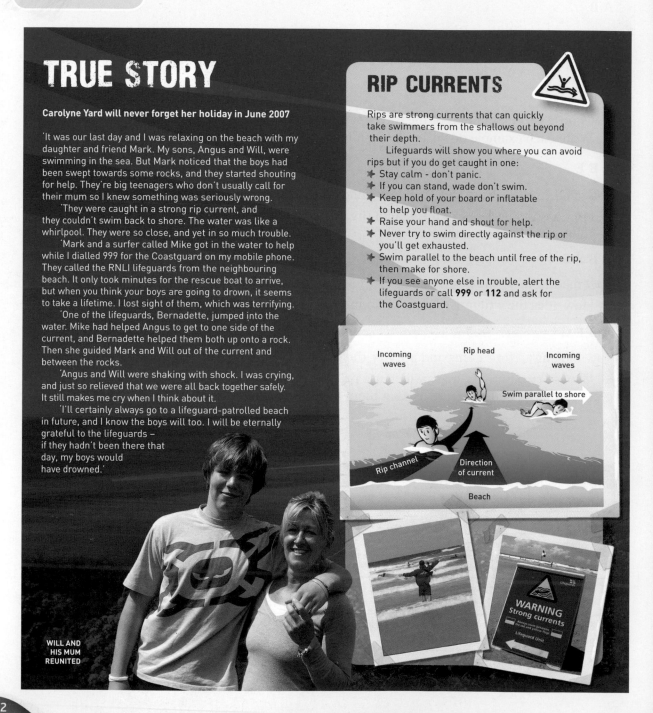

TRUE STORY

Carolyne Yard will never forget her holiday in June 2007

'It was our last day and I was relaxing on the beach with my daughter and friend Mark. My sons, Angus and Will, were swimming in the sea. But Mark noticed that the boys had been swept towards some rocks, and they started shouting for help. They're big teenagers who don't usually call for their mum so I knew something was seriously wrong.

'They were caught in a strong rip current, and they couldn't swim back to shore. The water was like a whirlpool. They were so close, and yet in so much trouble.

'Mark and a surfer called Mike got in the water to help while I dialled 999 for the Coastguard on my mobile phone. They called the RNLI lifeguards from the neighbouring beach. It only took minutes for the rescue boat to arrive, but when you think your boys are going to drown, it seems to take a lifetime. I lost sight of them, which was terrifying.

'One of the lifeguards, Bernadette, jumped into the water. Mike had helped Angus to get to one side of the current, and Bernadette helped them both up onto a rock. Then she guided Mark and Will out of the current and between the rocks.

'Angus and Will were shaking with shock. I was crying, and just so relieved that we were all back together safely. It still makes me cry when I think about it.

'I'll certainly always go to a lifeguard-patrolled beach in future, and I know the boys will too. I will be eternally grateful to the lifeguards – if they hadn't been there that day, my boys would have drowned.'

WILL AND HIS MUM REUNITED

RIP CURRENTS

Rips are strong currents that can quickly take swimmers from the shallows out beyond their depth.

Lifeguards will show you where you can avoid rips but if you do get caught in one:

✴ Stay calm – don't panic.
✴ If you can stand, wade don't swim.
✴ Keep hold of your board or inflatable to help you float.
✴ Raise your hand and shout for help.
✴ Never try to swim directly against the rip or you'll get exhausted.
✴ Swim parallel to the beach until free of the rip, then make for shore.
✴ If you see anyone else in trouble, alert the lifeguards or call **999** or **112** and ask for the Coastguard.

Incoming waves   Rip head   Incoming waves

Swim parallel to shore

Rip channel   Direction of current

Beach

WARNING
Strong currents

Item 2

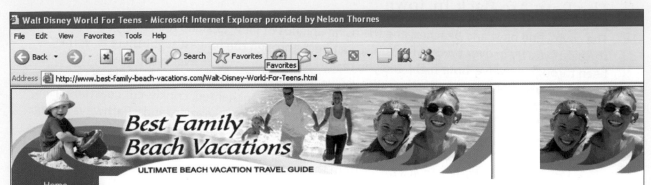

Walt Disney World For Teens - Microsoft Internet Explorer provided by Nelson Thornes

File   Edit   View   Favorites   Tools   Help

Back   Search   Favorites

Address   http://www.best-family-beach-vacations.com/Walt-Disney-World-For-Teens.html

Best Family Beach Vacations
ULTIMATE BEACH VACATION TRAVEL GUIDE

Home
Family Beach Blog
Family Destinations
All Inclusive Vacations
Beaches Resorts
Caribbean Vacations
Mexico Vacations
USA Vacations
Hawaii Vacations
Canada Vacations
South Pacific
Europe Vacations
Africa Vacations
South America
Disney Vacations

Walt Disney World For Teens

Walt Disney World for Teens? Wondering if your kids or teens are too 'old' to enjoy a Disney Vacation? Need to know what there is for them to do?

Can teens really have fun at a place like Walt Disney World? Absolutely! Actually, be prepared to have the time of your life. It's a safe place to assert some independence from your parents, a place you'll never forget. Here are some of the best experiences for teens at 'The Most Magical Place on Earth':

Walt Disney World for Teens – Have a Splashing Good Time at Disney's Water Parks

For a blast of a time, head to one of Disney's two water parks. Blizzard Beach has a melting alpine resort theme where chairlifts carry swimmers instead of skiers. It's a place for daredevils to challenge wild, rushing water and death-defying slides including the Summit Plummet, a 120-foot slide reaching speeds of 60 miles per hour. Those a bit less adventuresome will love Typhoon Lagoon, a tropical fantasyland offering a wave pool with the tallest simulated waves in the world as well as a chance to snorkel among tropical fish, leopard and nurse sharks, and picturesque coral at Shark Reef.

Walt Disney World for Teens – Live it Up at Downtown Disney

After the parks close hop on a bus from your Disney resort for a night on the town at Downtown Disney. Highlights include Disney Quest with five floors of interactive games, a 24-screen AMC Theater, a Cirque du Soleil show, and over 60 shops and restaurants.

Item 3

Item 4

The Boys Are Back In Town

The coves, and bays and beaches, and the rising uplands of New Zealand look oddly familiar from the air as you fly in over the Pacific. You've just been through the longest flight there is, you've been through a twelve-hour night and you really can't be sure you've ever had a life off the aircraft. You've got lost in some time slip, you've been ghosted by travel, as the writer has it. But then the waiting is over. In the dawn you look down to this enchanted, crinkle-cut coastline rising out of the Pacific Ocean. Tracks lead up the cliffs to smooth green grazing lands. Pathways zigzag up and down the gulleys; there are uplands and copses, and everything's shining underneath an ultramarine sky. And why does it look oddly familiar? It's exactly like the children's first sight of Never Never Land in *Peter Pan*. It's magic from the first moment you see it.

You're on the edge of the world, two thousand miles from any other city. There's the Antarctic down there and over the horizon there's Sydney. But down in Hawke's Bay, you can look eastwards, towards the rising sun, and there's nothing except the world's biggest, bluest ocean all the way until you hit Chile.

Simon Carr, *The Boys Are Back In Town*

Sample answers

You have one hour in which to read four texts and answer six questions. You need to work quickly and give focused answers. Look at the questions again and note how many marks each question is worth. If you do not complete all the questions, you lose a lot of marks.

Questions 1 and 2 test your ability to find information in a text to answer a question. If you get these right, you get 10 marks and are well on the way to a good grade. Re-read the questions carefully and check the notes you made in Activity 1. Make sure you have selected the correct number of things to enable you to get full marks.

Now check your choices against the following correct answers to work out your marks.

1 List **four** things that you **should** do if you get caught in a rip without a board or inflatable.

(*4 marks*)

1 mark for each of the following:

Stay calm.

If you can stand, wade.

Raise your hand and shout for help.

Swim parallel to the beach until free of the rip (then make your way to shore).

Check:
- Did you list four things?
- Did you notice that the question asked you for things you should do?
- Did you notice that the question referred to being without a board or inflatable?

2 List **six** different reasons why, according to this web page, teenagers might enjoy
Walt Disney World.   *(6 marks)*

1 mark for each of up to six of the following:

It's a safe place to assert independence.

It's a place you'll never forget.

It has two water parks.

Blizzard Beach has chairlifts that carry swimmers.

Summit Plummet has a 120-foot slide reaching
speeds of 60 miles per hour.

Typhoon Lagoon offers a wave pool with the tallest
simulated waves in the world.

You can snorkel at Shark Reef.

You can see tropical fish, leopard and nurse sharks
and picturesque coral at Shark Reef.

You can go to Downtown Disney at night.

Disney Quest has five floors of interactive games.

You can visit the 24-screen AMC Theatre or a Cirque
du Soleil show.

There are over 60 shops and restaurants.

Check:
- Did you list six reasons?
- Did you take your reasons from the web page?
- Did you think about what teenagers might enjoy?

3 Choose **three** examples of the way language is used for effect in this web page.
Write each example down and explain how each example is being used for effect.

(6 marks)

This asks you to select and write down three examples of language and to explain how the
language is being used for effect. You are awarded 1 mark for each example you write down
and 1 mark for each explanation of how the example is being used for effect. Two examples are
given below:

Example 1: Can teens really have fun at a place like
Walt Disney?

Explanation: The writer has used a question to
address the readers directly and to make them want
to know what Walt Disney offers for teenagers.

Example 2: death-defying slides

Explanation: The words 'death-defying' make the
slides sound dangerous and exciting as though you
are risking your life by going on them.

Check:
- Did you choose three examples?
- Did you explain how each example is being used for effect?

4   How has the designer of this leaflet organised the information and the pictures to have
     an impact on the reader?   (*8 marks*)

This is a completely different type of question. You have to decide which features of structure you will pick out and what you will say about those features. Your answer is worth 8 marks.

The following student achieved a mark of 5. The highlights show you what the student did well to gain these marks.

Read the response and the annotations:

There is a large picture of the forest with people swinging through the trees and walking on ropes. You can see all the trees and the things you can go on. Then there's another picture of a woman on one of the ropes and she is smiling. This makes you think that you would enjoy going there as there are lots of things to do and it looks like fun. The headline is at the top in large white font, which makes it stand out, and there's an exclamation mark to make you think you should do this. There's some sun shining through the trees so you think the weather will always be good there and you will want to go. Most of the words are in big orange circles and different bits of information are organised into different circles. There's not too much to read so you can find out what you need to know easily.

The green highlighting describes what is seen.

The pink highlighting explains and comments.

Examiner's comment

In order to gain higher marks, this student needed to show that he could:

- Make links between the written text and the pictures.
- Show awareness of the intended audience.
- Say something about the impact of the way the whole page is organised.

Activity

2 With a partner, think about the three bullet points listed in the examiner's comment. For each one, write a sentence that would help this student to gain 8 marks.

5 How does the writer use language to interest and inform the reader? *(8 marks)*

This is like Question 4. You have to decide what things you should write about. It's best to choose a few things that you can say something about, rather than a lot of things. In this question, you get most of the marks for the comments you make. Aim to write two good comments about language used to interest and two good comments about language used to inform. If you have more time at the end, you can add to your answer.

You are going to practise writing good comments. Here are some of the things you could select to write about:

Language to interest:
- Repeated use of the second-person pronoun 'you'.
- Use of adjectives, for example 'enchanted, crinkle-cut', 'smooth green grazing lands'.
- Comparison with 'the children's first sight of Never Never Land in Peter Pan'.

Language to inform:
- Details of what you see from the plane, for example 'The coves, and bays and beaches', 'Pathways zigzag up and down the gulleys'.
- Facts such as 'two thousand miles from any other city' and 'over the horizon there's Sydney'.

Here is a comment on the first one of these points:

The writer addresses the readers directly using the words 'you', 'you've' and 'you're'. He does this to help the reader imagine that it's them who are in the plane and seeing New Zealand for the first time. It makes the writing more personal and helps the reader to understand what the long journey is like. It also makes the description seem more real and helps the reader to have a clearer picture.

Activity

3 a Choose two other bullet points on which to write a comment. Think about what to say before writing your comment.

b Compare your comments with another student. Which ones do you think would gain the most marks? Why do you think this?

6 Choose **two** of these items which use presentational devices. Compare the ways presentational devices are used in them in order to interest the reader. *(8 marks)*

This question is different again; it asks you to choose two texts and to compare them. You are not comparing everything about them. You are asked to focus on comparing the ways presentational devices are used to interest the reader. Your choice of texts is important here. There is not a lot you could say about the use of presentational devices in Item 4 – this would be a bad choice. There is a lot you can say about Items 1, 2 and 3, so any two of these would be a good choice. In order to answer this question well, you need to think about:

- the presentational devices that are used in each item
- any similarities or differences between the use of the presentational devices in the two items
- how successful the presentational devices are in interesting the reader.

Activity

4

a With a partner, choose two of the items and make notes on each bullet point.

b Share your ideas with another pair. On a large piece of paper, map all the different things you could say in answer to sample question 6. Highlight the things you think would gain the most marks.

c Using your highlighted notes to help you, write an answer to sample question 6. Aim to spend ten minutes writing your answer.

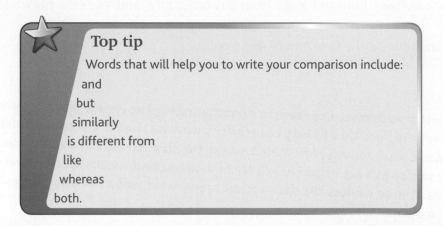

Top tip

Words that will help you to write your comparison include:

and

but

similarly

is different from

like

whereas

both.

Check your learning

In this chapter you have:

- learned how your reading skills will be tested in the exam
- studied sample questions and answers
- looked at how responses can be improved.

12

Making your reading skills count in the controlled assessment

Objectives

In this chapter you will:

learn more about how your reading skills are tested in the controlled assessment

explore the different options that are available to you

explore the different options that are available to you

look at some sample tasks and answers and consider how you can improve the answers.

What is controlled assessment?

During your GCSE course, the reading skills that you have developed during the first ten chapters of this section of the book will be tested by controlled assessment. What this will involve depends on whether you are studying GCSE English or GCSE English Language.

GCSE English

Controlled assessment title
Understanding creative texts

Mark value
20% = 40 marks

Texts you will have to study
- a play by Shakespeare
- a prose text from either a different culture or the English Literary heritage
- a poetry text from either a different culture or the English Literary heritage

Choice of task
One of:
- Themes and ideas
- Characterisation and voice

Planning and preparation:
You are allowed to spend time discussing the texts and task, and you may make brief notes which can be taken into the controlled assessment.

Time for writing:
Up to 4 hours

Expected length:
About 1600 words

GCSE English Language

Controlled assessment title:
Understanding written texts (extended reading)

Mark value:
15% = 30 marks

Texts you will have to study:
One of:
- a novel
- a collection of short stories
- a play
- a collection of poems
- a literary non-fiction text (e.g. biography or travel writing).

Choice of task topics:
One of:
- Themes and ideas
- Characterisation and voice

Planning and preparation:
You are allowed to spend time discussing the texts and task, and you may make brief notes which can be taken into the controlled assessment.

Time for writing:
Up to 4 hours

Expected length:
About 1200 words

You are allowed to take brief notes into the controlled assessment and to use a clean copy of the text.

You are not allowed:

- **Annotated versions of the texts:** copies of texts need to be 'clean'.
- **Pre-prepared drafts:** you must not write out a 'rough' version of your response and either seek advice about it or take it into the controlled assessment.
- To take your writing out of the controlled assessment room between sessions.

Your preparation may be based on discussion with other students of the text and task. You must spend time thinking about:

- key points you will make and the order you will make them in
- sections of the text you will focus on to make and develop your key points.

Identifying key sections of the text is an important part of your preparation. The best writing is always focused on important parts of the text. When you focus on sections you are more likely to comment on details of the writer's language. In your planning, therefore, you could make a note of the key sections of the text you wish to explore so that you do not waste time in the controlled assessment searching for appropriate passages.

In planning your response you are allowed to spend time reading, re-reading and discussing the texts. One of the best ways to approach any literary text is to discuss it with others but it is important to develop your personal response.

Introducing the tasks

There are two options for the controlled assessment task:

- **Themes and ideas:** this means you will need to write an essay in which you focus on one of the main ideas explored by the writer. For example, in *Romeo and Juliet* Shakespeare dramatises ideas about love and hate – you might be asked to develop your understanding of what the play shows about love and hate.
- **Characterisation and voice:** you might be asked to concentrate on how the writer presents one character or the relationship between characters in a text.

One of the most important differences between exams and controlled assessments is that you have quite a lot of time to prepare for the controlled assessment task. You will know the text and task – unlike in the exam – and you will be able to discuss and research the task in lessons before the controlled assessment.

To do well in the controlled assessment task you will need a good understanding of the Assessment Objectives for Reading. You will find a detailed breakdown of two of the objectives in Chapter 11, which focuses on the Reading part of the exam. However, there are another two parts Assessment Objectives for Reading which only apply to the controlled assessment.

GCSE English

Develop and sustain interpretations of writers' ideas and perspectives.

You need to be able to build up and extend your understanding of writers' ideas and intentions. In the exam you do not have enough time to analyse the ideas fully or in great depth but in the controlled assessment task you have quite a lot of time to prepare, explore and explain your ideas in detail.

Understand texts in their social, cultural and historical contexts.

'Contexts' refers to the kind of times and society in which the texts were written. For example, in the 17th Century Shakespeare wrote a play called *The Merchant of Venice*, which features a character who is Jewish. If you have some understanding of what life was like for Jewish people in Shakespeare's time, you will have a better grasp of different ideas explored in the play.

GCSE English Language

Develop and sustain interpretations of writers' ideas and perspectives.

You need to be able to build up and extend your understanding of writers' ideas and intentions. In the exam you do not have enough time to analyse the ideas fully or in great depth but in the controlled assessment task you have quite a lot of time to prepare, explore and explain your ideas in detail.

Sample tasks and answers

GCSE English

You have to write about three texts and have up to four hours in which to do so. This means each response will take little longer than one hour. When you plan you must take this into consideration. If you write at great length about two texts and only briefly about the third, you may lose marks.

You will be expected to:

- make an appropriate number of points for the time allowed
- select points and supporting evidence
- plan to finish your response in about one hour.

GCSE English Language

You have up to four hours to complete your ask but you only have to write about one text. This means that you have the time to explore a single text in more depth and detail than in GCSE English. It is important to break your task down into separate stages. For example, if you are responding to a play or novel you might decide to explore three or four separate sections of the text in detail and spend an hour on each section.

Here is a sample task based on the Theme topic area.

Explore the ways people's relationships with nature are developed in a text from the English Literary heritage.

Explore the ways means that you need to spend time identifying, explaining and evaluating:

- the writer's ideas
- some of the techniques used by the writer to develop their ideas.

In your response you need to show that you can select material from the text(s) which is suitable for the task. You should aim to use different parts of the text(s).

A text from the English Literary Heritage is a text written by an important writer who is no longer alive.

Activity

a Read Text A and look at the annotations, which explain
some of the ideas and techniques used.

Ⓐ

Below the Green Corrie

The mountains gathered round me
like bandits. Their leader
swaggered up close in the dark light,
full of threats, full of thunders.
But it was they who stood and delivered,
They gave me their money and their lives,
They filled me with mountains and thunders.
My life was enriched
with an infusion of theirs.
I clambered downhill through the ugly weather.
And when I turned to look goodbye
to those marvellous prowlers
a sunshaft had pierced the clouds
and their leader,
that swashbuckling mountain,
was wearing
a bandolier of light.

Norman MacCaig, 'Below the Green Corrie'

A simile is used here to give an impression of danger to the reader

The repetition adds to the sense of threat

The change in idea – that nature, rather than being threatening is actually positive and is developed through the use of the word 'enriched'

It is surprising to see things as usually unpleasant as 'prowlers' called 'marvellous. This helps to pull together the two main ideas of the poem so far – that mountains are threatening but also wonderful

The 'dark' and 'thunders' and 'ugly weather' of the early part of the poem is now replaced with light – again this reflects the change of idea in the poem

'But' introduces a change of idea developed in the rest of this line and the following two. 'stood and delivered' is a reference to the old-fashioned phrase 'stand and deliver' used by highwaymen when they were demanding money and valuables from their victims

An 'infusion' shows that the writer sees mountains as living things able to affect people

These two words return us to the idea of 'highwaymen' but using a word like 'swashbuckling' is romantic and glamorous, rather than threatening. A 'bandolier' is an ammunition belt usually worn across one shoulder – it is also associated with the stereotypical view of bandits and pirates

Here is an example of how one student planned their response to 'Below the Green Corrie':

- Introduction: the poem focuses on one feature of nature – mountains – and shows that the writer has both negative and positive feelings towards them.
- Explore lines 1 to 4 which suggest threat, use lines 2 and 4 for quotations. (5 minutes)
- Explore lines 5 to 10 in which the writer suggests positive feelings about the mountains. Use lines 5, 7 and 8 for quotations. (10 minutes)
- Explore lines 11 to 17 and explain how the writer's ideas about threat and wonder are explanded. Use line 12, 13 and 17 for quotations. (10 minutes)
- Conclusion: a precise answer to the question in the task. (5 minutes)

The timings are not meant to be exact but they give a rough indication of timing which should allow the student to finish the task. You will notice that the student has made a note of the lines he or she will select quotations from.

The plan approaches the poem in a logical way. To show understanding of structure, the student follows the sequence of ideas in the poem, for example, how the poem opens and ends.

Activity

2 Read Texts B and C, which are extracts from two students' responses to Text A. The task, remember, was to 'Explore the ways the writers' relationships with nature are developed in a text from the English Literary Heritage.'

Before you read the examiner's response to the two pieces, make up your own mind about which is the better of the two and list the qualities which make it better.

Ⓑ
Student 1

The poet does not like the mountains very much. He calls them 'bandits.' It sounds as if he is scared of them. This could be because mountains are very tall and high. Later in the poem I think the poet changes his mind because he says his life was 'enriched' by them. This means he has stopped being scared of them and now sees them as beautiful. As he climbs back downhill he is not afraid to say goodbye to them. The last word in the poem is 'light'. This gives a good impression of the mountains and it seems clear that he likes them now.

Ⓒ

Student 2

The writer's attitude to nature changes as the poem develops. At the start of the poem he finds nature threatening. He describes the mountains as 'bandits'. This idea that nature is threatening is repeated in the next few lines as he writes the mountains are 'full of threats'. He implies that mountains are dangerous places. However his attitude changes in the fifth line of the poem as he says the mountains, 'stood and delivered'. In olden days robbers would say, 'Stand and deliver!' to their victims as they demanded their valuables. The writer seems to be saying that the mountains aren't threatening at all, in fact they give things to people. He writes of the wealth he gets from mountains, 'My life was enriched' and says that he soaks something up from them like an 'infusion'. At the end of the poem it is interesting that the darkness and thunder of the opening lines has been replaced by 'a sunshaft'. It seems as though the mountains are shining some light into his life.

Teacher's comment: Student 1

The student shows some awareness of the writer's feelings towards the mountains. This is supported by the relevant quotation 'bandits'. The student is aware that the poet's feelings towards the mountains are mixed, again using a relevant textual reference 'enriched'. However the student could have displayed clearer understanding of the writer's use of language by exploring the effects of the word 'enriched' and by linking it to other words in the poem. The student needs to select more examples from the text for comment and explanation in order to demonstrate clear and consistent understanding.

Teacher's comment: Student 2

This response may be placed in a higher band than the first one. The student provides clear explanations of both the general idea of the poem – the different views of the mountains – and some comment on relevant details. The response begins with a clear focus on the key element of the task. Having made the statement that the writer's relationship with nature changes, the student logically examines the beginning of the poem. The first use of textual detail – 'The mountains gathered round me / like bandits.' Is relevant and appropriate although there could be more comment on it. The student identifies that the writer is using words which suggest 'threat', a point which is relevant and clear but a little obvious considering that the word 'threatening' is used in the poem. However he does emphasise the sense of danger which is implied in the poem.

The student clearly points out the change in writer's attitude and bases this understanding on an appropriate textual detail, 'stood and delivered', which is well explained by a comment about the cultural context of these words – that they are from an old highwayman expression. This explanation is quite well developed, although, the comments about the ending of the poem are a little rushed; they could have been further explained in more detail.

Storm in the Black Forest

Now it is almost night, from the bronzey soft sky
jugfull after jugfull of pure white liquid fire, bright white
tipples over and spills down,
and is gone
and gold-bronze flutters bent through the thick upper air.
And as the electric liquid pours out, sometimes
a still brighter white snake wriggles among it, spilled
and tumbling wriggling down the sky:
and then the heavens **cackle** with **uncouth** sounds.
And the rain won't come, the rain refuses to come!
This is the electricity that man is supposed to have mastered
chained, **subjugated** to his use!
supposed to!

D.H. Lawrence, 'Storm in the Black Forest'

Key terms

Cackle: Harsh high-pitched sound or laugh (often suggesting pleasure at the misfortune of another).

Uncouth: Behaving in an ill-mannered, unrefined way (being awkward or clumsy).

Subjugated: Brought under control.

Activity

3 Read Text E, part of a student's reponse to Text D, the poem 'Storm in the Black Forest'. What advice would you give to the student about how to improve their response? Think about how well they focus on the key words in the task and develop their ideas.

The writer is describing a storm in the Black Forest one evening, 'Now it is almost night,'. In the first five lines he describes the lightning as though someone is pouring it down from the sky, 'Jugfull'. He points out how very white the lightning is because he repeats the word.

In the middle of the poem he changes from describing the lightning as being a liquid. Instead he calls it a 'snake'. This shows that his feelings for nature aren't very good because snakes aren't very nice. He also mentions the thunder and makes it sound like a witch, 'the heavens cackle with uncouth sounds'.

In the end he shows that people think they are wonderful, that they can control anything but in reality they can't control things like the power of lightning because he says 'man is supposed to have mastered' electricity, the phrase 'supposed to' shows that the writer thinks man hasn't been able to control nature, nature is still all powerful.

Check your learning

In this chapter you have:

- learned about how your reading skills are tested in the controlled assessment
- learned more about the ways you can achieve high marks in this part of the course.

Writing is a skill that you probably have been learning ever since you started school … so why a whole section about it now, when you're working on your GCSE?

Getting started

Discuss with a partner how you feel about the following:

- Explain what you like and/or dislike about writing.
- Why do you think writing is considered to be such an important skill?

Aims of the Writing section

The qualification you are studying will equip you to use your writing skills in a range of situations, including:

- school and college courses after GCSEs
- work-based learning
- personal and business communications such as letters and emails
- recording ideas in an organised and clear way.

There will be opportunities for you to revise the knowledge you already have, but also to extend that knowledge and develop it in new directions. Working with other students, you will be encouraged to try out new ideas and help them to improve their writing too. You will read extracts from texts which will demonstrate how professional writers use language for particular effects – and then try out creating those effects yourself.

Does this all sound a bit 'too much'?

Don't worry, you will not be expected to do all of this straightaway. The tasks are intended to help you gradually improve your ability to tackle different forms of writing and work on each aspect so you have the chance to build up your confidence.

Basics

Writing in sentences is one of the most important skills you need to be successful in for English. However, you may still not be sure that you have got this quite right. You will have the chance to practise writing in a variety of sentence styles and experimenting with the ways that sentences can be constructed.

You will also have the chance to look at how words are used to create different feelings and impressions for the reader. This work with words will help you to change the way you write to meet different tasks for the assessments you will have to do.

Assessments

The chapters each address differing aspects of the GCSE course. At the start of each chapter, you will know what area you are going to be working on and what you should be able to achieve by the time you have finished the different tasks.

There are two forms of assessment:

- controlled assessment
- exam.

The Writing section will help you to prepare for both of these types of assessment.

13

Communicate clearly

Objectives

In this chapter you will:

practise making your writing clear to a reader.

revise using correct sentences, punctuation and verb tenses.

Communicating clearly in writing is a skill that you will need not only for your exams, but also when you go to college or work. This chapter explains some of the skills that will help you to make sure readers understand exactly what you are writing.

What makes a sentence a sentence?

To write clearly, it is important that you use sentences. Look at these examples:

Boys prefer football.

Sheep pretend carpet.

pink highlighting Subject

blue highlighting Verb

Both examples look similar, but only one of them makes sense.

A sentence has to:

- have a **verb**
- have a **subject**
- make sense.

> **Key terms**
>
> **Verb:** a word that shows an action or state. For example, jump, walk, think, am.
>
> **Subject:** a topic which is being described, discussed or written about.

Activity

1

a Copy the following examples and use two different colours to underline the verb and the subject in each example, then tick each one that makes sense. These are sentences.

- The dogs ran wild.
- Mobiles swim horizon.
- Police swarmed over the estate.
- Computers swooped down chairs.
- Milk dives on ice.
- Tea was on the table.

b Write four examples of your own. Two should be correct sentences and two should be nonsense ones. Swap your work with another student, and try to spot which two are correct sentences.

Using punctuation to make sentences clear

It is important to remember that a sentence contains a complete idea or piece of information. For example, read the following sentences:

> The party began at five. Fifteen children had been invited.
> A clown was coming to entertain them.

Each sentence gives the reader new information. Each sentence starts with a capital letter and ends with a full stop.

You also need to remember that sentences need to be **punctuated** correctly. This involves, at least, a capital letter at the start of each sentence and a full stop at the end.

Key terms

Punctuation: the marks and letters used to show how text should be read. Different marks mean different things.

Activity

2

a Revise your knowledge of basic sentence punctuation by rewriting the following paragraph and adding capital letters and full stops in the correct places. Hint: there are four sentences.

> the cup match started at three o'clock both teams had been training hard for weeks and wanted to win the fans were keen to see the trophy won by their team this match was the most important of the season

b Of course, full stops and capital letters are not the only types of punctuation that can be used in sentences. Check what else you remember by copying out the following table and reordering the words to match the correct symbol with its name and what it is used for. The first one (comma) has been done for you.

Symbol	Name	What it is used for
,	comma	Breaks up a sentence and shows a pause.
" "	brackets	Used after something is shouted, or a command or a sudden cry.
!	apostrophe	Shows a question is being asked.
'	capital letters	Indicates what someone says or a quote.
?	speech marks	Used in pairs. May go around words which give a further comment in the sentence.
( )	exclamation mark	Shows where words have been left out.
…	question mark	Used at the end of a sentence.
.	elilipsis	Shows a letter or letters have been missed.
R	full stop	Can be called 'upper case'. Used to begin sentences and names.

3

a Read the sentences below. Using your knowledge of punctuation, rewrite them using the correct punctuation so that they make sense. Hint: you should use four lots of speech marks, two question marks, an exclamation mark, two commas, five full stops, ten capital letters and four apostrophes.

> what time does the show start tonight asked jenna
>
> i think its about seven but it might be later replied sara
>
> seven i cant be ready by then
>
> youll have to try snapped sara though she knew she was wasting her breath jenna couldnt ever be ready on time

b With a partner, continue the conversation for four more lines. Check to make sure you are using the right punctuation and setting it out correctly. (For example, every time a new/different person speaks, a new line should be started.)

Why are commas not enough?

Sometimes it may seem easier to keep using commas if you are a bit unsure about where full stops should go. However, this can make text quite hard to read and understand. Read Text A, written by a student as part of a film review.

Ⓐ Van Helsing is about a vampire hunter, he tracks down monsters and then gets rid of them, he works for a load of church people, who are a bit weird and want him to catch Dracula, so he goes to a town which has a problem with lots of vampires, and then he meets a girl, who has a brother, who is turning into a werewolf, and I think it is good to watch because the film has lots of fights.

When you read this review, although you have an idea of what the writer is trying to say, it is confusing and unclear because it is not punctuated properly. It could be improved by changing some of the commas for full stops, but also by changing some of the words used as there are quite a few repeated words.

Activity

4

a With a partner, read the next paragraph of the review (Text B) and discuss how you could change it to improve what the writer is trying to say. If you have a copy of the text, use coloured pens to:

- underline words and phrases that you think are repeated too often
- use arrows to show where you would move sentences
- circle commas you think should be replaced with other punctuation.

b Rewrite the passage to make it clearer. Check that you have:

- replaced some commas with other punctuation
- cut out some words
- replaced some words with other words that are clearer
- reorganised some of the sentences to make it read better.

(B)

There are some vampire women who fly about and kidnap people, and it has loads of SEX which make it scary in places. Van Helsing has to go to the castle and rescue the people who are kidnapped, and the girl goes with him, because she wants to rescue her brother, but it's too late for him as Dracula has got him. The women all have weird babies in pods that are all slimy and horrible, and Van Helsing has to get round them as well. The SFX works well to make it seem spooky in the castle and there are lots of weird machines Dracula is trying to use.

Using the right verb tense

Another aspect of writing that can sometimes be confusing is **verb tense**. You know that every sentence needs a verb, but in most texts the verbs also need to be in the same tense. If you read a text that does not have verbs which agree (this means that they all express the same time – past, present or future), it again can make it hard to understand.

Key terms

Verb tense: the way a verb shows the different times at which events take place. For example, 'he was here' is the past tense because it is something that has already happened.

Activity

5

Check you know the three main tenses and their forms. Match the following tenses to some of their common forms and record your answers.

a Present	**i** we will be going / I shall find / she may be able
b Past	**ii** I see / we are here / he helps me
c Future	**iii** you were leaving / I had no chance / you have been

a Read Text C from an autobiography written by a Year 9 student. You can probably tell that the verb tenses are mixed up. She is using both past and present tense. Write out the extract twice – first in past tense and then again using present tense.

C

When I was about eight, Polly and I went for a walk into the woods. We heard that there was a haunted house there so we are going to look at it.

When we saw it, we thought it must be empty. The windows are all broken and the paint looked messy. The garden is overgrown. The door was hanging off the hinges. I want to go in but Polly says 'I'm scared there's a ghost in there' so I went in on my own.

b With a partner, compare your versions of rewritten Text C. Check that all the verbs are now in the same tense. Discuss any differences between your word choices.

Background

Autobiography is something that many celebrities write, to tell their fans about their life and how they have achieved fame. The best autobiographies do not include every little detail from a person's life, but put in the events that have made them the person they are.

Check your learning

Writing part of your own autobiography is a task that you could be set as part of your coursework. Read the background information on autobiographies before completing the task below.

You are going to plan and write an extract from your own life story, using your skills in:

- organising words into clear sentences
- using punctuation to help the reader follow your ideas
- using the correct verb tenses.

a Before you start writing, take some time to record major events that have happened to you. You could use a mind map, a timeline, paragraph outline or list. From your record, choose an event that you remember clearly and you feel has had an impact on your life. This could be a happy or sad memory, something that happened when you were a small child or something that happened more recently. It may involve family members or friends.

b Focus on that one event and make some notes about the things you recall. These could include what you saw or heard, what you could smell or how you felt. Include some details about any other people who were involved. Write these notes quite briefly, just to remind you of what to include. The example on page 93 shows how one student planned their writing in note form:

> Birth of brother – I was four – Nan looked after me, baked buns with her – slept at their house, felt like a holiday – went to visit in hospital – smelt funny – baby brother real red looking, lots of black hair. Got a present for being good. Didn't like him being at home – he cried a lot. Wanted mum to take him back.

c Describe to another student what you remember about your event and how it has affected you. Listen to their event too. Take some time to ask questions that will help you understand how they felt, what they saw and how their life has been changed since that time.

d After sharing your accounts, add any more details you have recalled to your notes. Then write out the account in full. Try to show how the event has affected your life. You may need to explain how you felt at the time and how you feel now.

e Once you have finished writing, check your work to make sure:

- you have written in sentences
- you have used correct punctuation in the right places
- your verb tenses are correct.

f Exchange your work with your partner and read through their account. Discuss with them any aspects that could be improved or made clearer. Edit your work after listening to their suggestions.

Stretch yourself

Some people in the public eye do not write their autobiography. Other people may write about them instead, either with or without the help of the famous person. This is called a biography. Biographies can also be written about historical figures who have been dead for many years.

Having written about your own life, use these skills you have practised to write part of a biography of someone else. Aim to write no more than 500 words. This could be a person who you know something about, for example a celebrity, or it could be someone you admire even though they are not famous – perhaps your grandfather. Use the following points to help you:

- Focus on a particular part of their life.
- You may be able to research some facts if you choose a real person.
- Make sure you continue to apply what you have learnt about writing clearly.

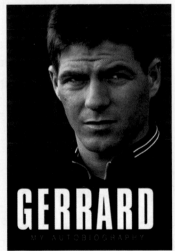

14

Say what you mean

What is the purpose of a text?

The purpose of a text is the reason for which it has been written. Look at this text extract:

FIRE PROCEDURES ◄ — Title of the notice

If the fire alarm sounds, leave the building by the nearest fire exit. Do not use the lift.

— A situation which might make some people panic

— Instructions

This text has one main purpose: to explain exactly what to do, and what not to do, if a fire starts in the building. Texts can have more than one purpose. These might include to:

- sell
- inform
- entertain
- describe
- persuade
- instruct.

Activity

1

a Read the Milkodrops bag (Text A). It has more than one purpose. Use the bullet points above to help you identify and write down three different purposes of the wrapper.

b Write some of the text of a wrapper that would be used to persuade people to buy one of the products in the following list.
Aim to write between 10 and 20 words. Choose from this list:

- A fruit drink.
- A box of chocolates.
- A packet of crisps.
- A packet of frozen peas.

c Compare your text with another student. Decide which is the most persuasive and why.

d Using what you have learnt, write the text for the wrapper of another product from the list above. Aim to write between 10 and 20 words and make your writing as persuasive as possible.

Who is the audience of a text?

Audience means the intended reader or readers of the text. Look again at Text A. Parts of it are written for different intended readers. The Nutritional Information Table is intended to be read by adults. You can tell this because the words used are to do with food contents. It also refers to the nutritional needs of a child, but the words are too difficult for small children to read.

Activities

2

a Who is the intended reader of the cartoon? How can you tell?

b Who is the intended reader of the Milkodrops recipe ingredients? How do you know?

3

a Write three sentences that would go on the wrapper of a new brand of sugar-free sweets. One sentence should target young children, one sentence should target teenagers and one sentence should target parents. Each sentence should be about ten words. Do not label the sentences, and remember to vary your words for each audience.

b Compare your sentences with another student. Can they work out which sentence targets which audience from the way you have used words?

c Next, write the text for a 50-word magazine advertisement for the new sweets. Your target audience is parents. Plan your ideas and think about the kinds of words you should use before starting to write. You have two purposes:

- to let people know about these new sweets
- to persuade the reader to buy them.

As you have seen, writers vary the words they use and how they use them to suit the purpose and audience. Look at Text B, which is a recipe. The writer's purpose is to give instructions on how to make shortcrust pastry. The audience is readers who want to make the pastry. The writing has clear, identifiable features, which are annotated for you.

Sentences start with a directive

Sentences are numbered to show the correct order

(B) **Making shortcrust pastry**

1) Cut up 50g of margarine and 50g of white fat. Place the fats in a bowl.

2) Add 200g of plain flour and a pinch of salt.

3) Rub fat into flour until it resembles breadcrumbs.

Sentences are short and factual

Punctuation is limited to capital letters and full stops

Activity k!

4 Read the following texts (Texts C–F). Then copy and complete this table, identifying purpose, audience and language features. Text B (the recipe) has been done for you as an example.

Type of text	Purpose	Audience	Language features
B Recipe	Give instructions on how to make shortcrust pastry	Someone who wants to know how to make shortcrust pastry	• Uses directions • Short sentences • Instructions numbered • Capital letters and full stops
C Postcard			
D TV listing			
E CD review			
F Advert			

Postcard

Ⓒ

Arrived in Pila this morning. Coach journey was a pain. Slopes look amazing! We'll be on the ski lift as soon as it opens tomorrow! Hotel OK – handy for town, clean, but not luxurious.

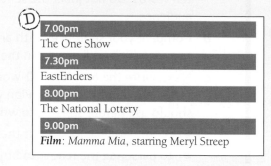

Ⓓ

7.00pm
The One Show
7.30pm
EastEnders
8.00pm
The National Lottery
9.00pm

Film: *Mamma Mia*, starring Meryl Streep

Ⓔ

Listening to the new CD release from Brenda Briars was like stepping back in time. Forget all the recent disasters (like the rapping with Creep Catt) and think about her early poptastic singles! I expected this album to be different – and Brenda hasn't disappointed. … ★★★★★

Ⓕ

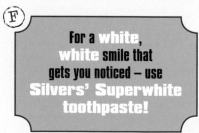

For a white, white smile that gets you noticed – use Silvers' Superwhite toothpaste!

Activity

5 Use what you have learned from examining these texts to help you write the following:

a Imagine you have gone abroad on holiday, perhaps for the first time. Write a postcard to a grandparent telling them about where you are staying, what you have been doing and what you think about the holiday. Write between 30 and 50 words.

b Write a short CD review for a music magazine for teenagers. Choose a CD you know and like. Explain what sort of music it is, how it compares with other music by the same/similar bands and why you like it. Write between 80 and 100 words.

Choosing the right sort of language

We use language in different ways in writing to suit our purpose and audience. At times, we use language more informally than at others. We do this when we speak as well as when we write. Look at the example in the cartoons below.

When speaking to a friend, you may use language more informally than if you were speaking to the headteacher.

Most speakers find that they change what they say and how they say it depending on who they are talking to. It is the same with writing. It can be either formal or informal:

Formal:
- has a serious purpose
- is polite
- uses **Standard English**.

Informal:
- is chatty and casual
- seems more like speech
- may use **slang** and abbreviations.

> **Key terms**
>
> **Standard English**: the variety of English usually used by public figures (such as the Queen and newsreaders). It is not limited to a particular region and can be spoken with any accent.
>
> **Slang**: words or phrases that are used when speaking or writing informally, often linked with certain regions or used by certain groups of people.

We vary the formality of our writing depending on what we are writing, why we are writing it and who we are writing for.

Texting

Text messaging, or texting, is the name given to the usually informal exchange of short written messages between mobile phones. It is a relatively new form of communication and young people tend to be experts at it.

Text language is developing and changing rapidly and has distinct features:

Words are often abbreviated and/or letters are changed – for example Thnx (thanks)

Single letters are used to replace whole words for example (tea)

Thnx 4 pressie. Goin 2 b @ home 4 t .Can u ring me l8r plz ☺

Numbers are used to replace words or parts of words – for example 4 (for)

Symbols are used – for example @ (at), and emoticons are used to convey feelings – for example ☺

Punctuation is not standard and may not be used at all – for example, no? (question mark)

Sentences are usually short

Activity

6

a Work in pairs. List three or more reasons why text messages are so popular.

b When might it not be appropriate to text a message? Explain why.

c Many older people do not know how to text. They need a lot of help if they are to understand and use text language. Write an explanation of how to text for older people. Include ideas about the benefits of texting and instructions about how to do it. You can use diagrams, charts and bullet points in your explanation.

d Read another student's explanation. Is it clear and helpful? Is it suitable for audience and purpose? Tell them what you think or write a comment at the end.

Informal and formal emails

Another common form of electronic communication is email. Emails are generally used in workplaces as an efficient way of passing on information quickly. They can be formal or informal, depending on their purpose or audience.

Activity

7

a Read Text H, which is an informal email sent between two workmates. The annotations explain some of its features.

b Write Stella's reply, using some or all of the features of informal emails shown in Text H. Stella needs to mention in her reply to Jon that:

- she won't be in the office the next day
- she's got two good ideas for saving money
- she could make a meeting at 2 pm the following day.

c Annotate your email, showing the features you have used.

First names only are used, with no other greeting (for example, Dear …) or ending phrase (for example, Yours truly)

Using question marks shows that suggestions are being made instead of orders being given, which is friendlier

 (H)

→ Stella

Have you time for a quick meeting tomorrow? Need to talk about new ideas for how to save money (could start by sacking a few round here)! Try to bring some suggestions with you? Let me know when will be OK for you asap.

Jon

Sentences are brief, but to the point – they don't waste words that are not needed, a bit like notes

Some use of jokes and slang make the tone seem chatty and friendly

Activity

8

a The email in Text I was sent by the same person as Text H. In it, Jon writes to his senior officer and adopts a more formal style. List three or more ways in which the style is different to the more informal email in Text H.

(I)

> Mrs Rashid,
>
> Thank you for inviting a member of my staff to the next finance meeting. I will be sending Stella O'Dowd. Could you let me know how long the meeting will last? I am rather short staffed at the moment and would like Stella to come back here afterwards.
>
> Will you need her to bring any figures or data? If you let me know, I will arrange to have the printouts ready.
>
> Regards,
>
> Jon Chambers

b Write a reply to this email as if you were Mrs Rashid. First, decide on the details you need to include in your email. Aim to use a formal style in your reply.

Formal letters

Formal letters can be sent electronically or by post. One situation in which a formal letter would be appropriate is a letter of complaint.

Activity

9

Read this formal letter of complaint (Text J) on page 100. To help you identify the features of a formal letter, match the lettered features below to the correct number in the letter. You could record your findings in a table like this:

a Addresses recipient.

b Writer's address and postcode.

c Ends with 'Yours faithfully' and writer's full name.

d Address of business to which complaint is directed.

e Uses first person to make complaint more personal.

f Organised into paragraphs .

g Date.

1	2	3	4	5	6	7

15 Waterdale Grove
Henley-by-Derwent
DW17 5TM ❶

3rd March, 2010 ❷

Games4All
Comber Industrial Park
Twillingston
Bucks
BC4 8HG ❸

Dear Sir or Madam, ❹

I ❺ am writing to complain about a game which I bought last week at one of your shops. I can't return it there as I was only visiting the city for the day and live too far away to just go back with this one thing.

I paid £35.99 for 'Break-out'. I had saved up for this from my weekend job and looked forward to playing it. ❻

I was really disappointed when I tried to use it on my console as, almost at once, I got an error message. The disc wouldn't run properly and I couldn't find any info about how to make it work. I can't use the Internet as I can't afford it at the moment so I could not find any help there either. All the other games I have work fine, so it cannot be a problem with the console.

I'm sending the disc and case back to you. I would like a replacement that works please and if that is not possible, I'd like a refund of what I paid and the cost of posting it.

I look forward to hearing from you.

Yours faithfully, ❼

Jo Walters

Check your learning 🔊

Use what you have learnt in this chapter to write a formal letter of complaint, to be sent via email or post.

You are going to complain about the way you were treated in a restaurant you visited for a friend's birthday. The waiter was unhelpful and didn't pay you much attention, even though you had said it was a birthday treat. The service was slow and you waited a long time between courses. You think you were treated badly because you were teenagers.

Before you start, think about:

● Purpose: what you want to happen as a result of writing.
● Audience: who you will be writing to (the manager/owner of the restaurant).
● Content: what points you want to make.
● Organisation: how you will sequence the points you want to make.
● Language: how you will choose words appropriate to a formal letter.
● Tone: how you can make sure your letter is polite but firm.
● Form: the features of a formal letter that you will need to use.

When you have finished your letter, compare it with another student's. Decide which letter is most effective and why.

15

Building paragraphs

What does 'organised' mean to you?

Are you an organised person? Can you sort out what to do in the best order to get the right result?

Activity

1

a Read this list of chores that have to be done. Put them into an order that would help you get them done as quickly as possible.

- Hoover room.
- Fetch shopping.
- Wash clothes for school and going out.
- Finish homework.
- Walk dog.
- Empty waste bin.
- Tidy room.

b Share your ideas with another student. Compare your reasons for the order you would do them in. Which one of you seems to be better organised?

It is important to plan your writing for English tasks, just as you need to plan how best to do essential jobs. You may have learnt about ways to plan already.

Activity

2

a With a partner, look at these ways you might choose to plan your writing:

Spider 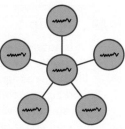　　Bulleted list 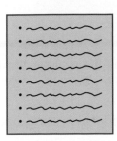　　Table 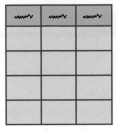　　Tree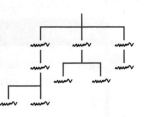

Activity

Discuss which of these would be suitable to use for writing:

- about a science experiment
- about a hobby or interest
- a short story
- directions to go somewhere
- about something you have read
- an account of an event.

b Share your ideas with another pair. Decide between you which two methods you think are the most useful. Discuss the reasons for your choice and record your ideas.

Creating a plan

A simple plan of what you intend to write before you start will save you time and worry later on in a task (this is important for coursework, controlled assessments and exams). For example, you may be set the task of writing a section of your autobiography.

The first step is to consider the purpose and audience for your writing, and then decide which form of writing will be most suitable.

For this task your audience is likely to be an adult (teacher). You will be writing information and description, so the form most suitable will be prose, written in the first person (that is, from the point of view of 'I' or 'we'). You should aim to use a plan that will help you jot down ideas quickly, see the Top tip for some suggestions.

Top tip

Plan suggestions:

■ You could write down a list of events from your childhood that you remember clearly and then choose two to write about in detail.

■ You may have a very clear memory of one thing that happened to you, so you could use a spidergram to develop your recall of the event.

■ A timeline may help you to sort events into the order in which they happened before selecting the ones that had the biggest impression upon you.

■ Paragraph outlines would help you make sure you were organising your ideas in a way that made sense, and it would give you a structure for your writing.

Activity

3

a Choose a planning method from the Top tip suggestions to create a plan for writing a section of your autobiography.

b Spend about five minutes writing a brief plan using that method.

c Share your plan with another student. Compare how you have each organised your ideas in the plans.

Top tip

It is not a good idea to try and write about your whole life in one assignment. If working on a similar task, you are better writing in a lot of detail about **one** event in your life, rather than writing very little about lots of events.

How to sequence information

You may make hot drinks at home. The way you do this will depend on whether you like tea or coffee, with milk or sugar. However you choose to make the drink, you will have had to use organisational skills to decide on the order in which you will do it. You need to use similar organisational skills to sort information in a text.

> **Key terms**
>
> **Sequence:** the order in which something is done or events happen; the way actions are carried out in a specific way.

Activity

a With a partner, read Text A, which has been mixed up. Put the paragraphs into a better sequence so that it makes sense to a reader.

b Compare your results with another pair.

Making an omelette

❶ Lastly, when the omelette and cheese mixture is firm to the touch, remove from the pan and serve.

❷ Pour in the egg mixture over the frying onions, and with a fork lightly stir it round so it starts to cook and becomes firmer. Make sure it does not stick to the sides and bottom as it will burn.

❸ Next, break the eggs into a deep bowl and whisk. Then add the milk and continue whisking. Add the salt and pepper at this stage.

❹ Add the chopped onions to the warmed fat. Cook them lightly until they start to turn brown.

❺ Set the egg mixture to one side. Chop the onion into small pieces and grate the cheese.

❻ Sprinkle the cheese over the mixture before it becomes too firm. For added flavour, you could place the pan under a grill for several minutes until the surface starts to turn brown and the cheese will bubble.

❼ Firstly, gather your ingredients. Use olive oil or butter for frying. Allow two eggs per person, plus milk, onions and cheese. You may wish to season with salt and pepper.

❽ Take your omelette pan (or frying pan) and place on a warm – not hot – ring. Pour in a dessertspoon of olive oil or drop in a lump of butter. Allow the fat to warm and coat the surface of the pan.

Discuss:

● any difficulties you found with the task

● how the words used provided clues about which sentence followed which

● why it would matter if the sequence was wrong when you tried to follow the recipe.

How to organise ideas in a whole text

When you write you need to use paragraphs. Sometimes students, and even adults, become confused about where paragraphs should end or start. When you change the subject, the time or the speaker, you should begin a new paragraph. Paragraphs help the reader to follow and understand the writer's ideas.

Background

You can show a new paragraph in two different ways. Usually when writing by hand, you should start a new line and leave a gap (called an indentation) before you start writing. Usually when writing using a computer, you should leave a blank line between paragraphs.

The length of a paragraph depends on whether you have included all you want to say on a subject. Some paragraphs are only one sentence long. Others are much longer and contain several sentences about the same subject.

Activity

5 With a partner, read Text B. The student who wrote it has not used paragraphs. The teacher has indicated where a new paragraph should have started with the symbol //. For each new paragraph indicated decide if there is:

- a change of subject
- a change of time
- a new speaker.

(B) The holiday started off well. The flight was on time and the airport wasn't too crowded. //When we arrived at the other end though it was a different story. Trouble started when we tried to pick up our luggage off the carousel. Someone was already shouting, 'What's happened to my suitcase? This was brand new!' The staff there were trying to explain, but no one was really listening; they were too busy complaining. //Look at the state of this! 'Mine is worse, have you seen it?' //By the time we got out of the airport with everything sorted it felt like we'd been in there for hours. Then we had to try and get a taxi.

Text B is all about the start of the holiday and the student has sequenced his ideas appropriately. However, as you can see from the relatively short paragraphs, there is very little development of the ideas. The text is simple and easy to follow but doesn't give the reader any more than the basic details.

Developing details in a paragraph

Organising ideas into paragraphs is the first step. You need to do more. Here, you will learn how to develop ideas within a paragraph.

1   Start with a topic sentence, which shows the main subject of the paragraph. For example:

> Being able to cook for yourself is an important life skill.

2   Add more detailed information about your point. This should give the reader a better understanding of the main point, not introduce a new idea. For example:

> This means more than being able to open and heat up a tin of beans or put a frozen meal into the microwave.

3   Show your reader more of what you mean by including anecdotes to prove your topic sentence is true. This gives a realistic example of what you are talking about:

> I know when I left home I could do little more than boil an egg and had to learn how to cook 'from scratch' – or risk starving!

4   Give facts to support the point you are making. These can be facts that you have researched or 'made-up' to make your point. For example:

> Ninety-five per cent of young people should have done Food Technology at school, but many still don't know how to prepare a basic meal.

5   Provide reasons which back up your topic sentence. For example:

> Having a balanced diet is critical to health for everyone, but being able to cook also means you can entertain friends and family as well as making sure you live well.

All of these together create a paragraph that is more interesting for a reader and also shows you can develop your ideas clearly and consistently. Read through the whole paragraph (Text C).

(C)

Being able to cook for yourself is an important life skill. This means more than being able to open and heat up a tin of beans or put a frozen meal into the microwave. I know when I left home I could do little more than boil an egg and had to learn how to cook 'from scratch' – or risk starving! Ninety-five per cent of young people should have done Food Technology at school, but many still don't know how to prepare a basic meal. Having a balanced diet is critical to health for everyone, but being able to cook also means you can entertain friends and family as well as making sure you live well.

Activity

6

a Choose one of the topic sentences below and develop it into a longer paragraph by using the five steps outlined on page 105.

- Computer games are stopping children from being physically active.
- Mobile phones are an essential part of life nowadays.
- Students should be allowed to leave school at 15 if they have a job to go to.

b Compare your paragraph with another student. Check that:

- the paragraph develops the topic sentence
- the ideas are linked.

Check your learning

a Spend five minutes thinking about what you have learnt in this chapter. Ask yourself the following questions:

- What methods can I use to plan my writing?
- What do I now understand about sequencing sentences now?
- Why is it important to plan my writing?
- When should I start a new paragraph?
- How can I develop the detail in my paragraphs?

b Share your responses with a student or small group. Discuss the differences in how you will organise your ideas from now on.

16

Word play

What is vocabulary?

The word 'vocabulary' means all the words used in English. It can also refer to those words that are linked with a particular subject or topic. Think about the subjects that you study. Each subject will have specific words that you need to learn to use. For example, words like 'calculate', 'average', 'algebra' and 'graph' are usually associated with Maths, so they are part of the Maths vocabulary.

Activities

1 a Look at the words listed below. Group them according to the subject you would most associate them with. Some words may fit into more than one area, so you can use them more than once.

Words:

settlement	experiment	rhyme	game	food
evaluate	environment	mat	forensic	image
athletic	continent	material	poem	organism
swimming	measure	housing	chemical	narrator

Subjects:

PE	Geography	ICT	English	Science

b Compare your ideas with another student. What differences can you find in the ways you have each grouped the words?

2 a Read the following sentences. What are the different meanings of the word 'room' in the following sentences?

> He found the room he wanted at the end of a corridor.
> He found room for dessert at the end of his meal.

b Look at the list below. For each word, write two sentences that show how the word can have different meanings

- bat
- creep
- book.

c Try to think of more examples where the meaning changes depending on how the word is used. Challenge another student to use the words you have chosen in two sentences which show the different meanings.

The meanings of words may vary depending on which subject they are used in. For example, a 'mat' is something you land on in PE, but it can also be a small piece of fabric on which you place your mouse in ICT. The precise meaning of a word depends on when and how it is being used.

How can word choice change meaning?

The English language has a large number of words that mean similar things. These are called **synonyms**. For example, walk, stroll, amble and stride are all synonyms. They all describe the ways someone could move, but each one has a slightly different meaning.

By trying out different words with similar meanings, you can subtly change the meaning of a sentence.

Imagine a father who wants to get the attention of his child. The words below show you some of the ways he could do this:

- Screech.
- Shout.
- Call.
- Bellow.

Each of these words gives the reader a different impression of how the father speaks to the child.

Key terms

Synonym: a word or phrase that means the same, or almost the same, as another word.

Activity

 3   The example above uses verbs, but it is possible to make similar choices when using **adjectives**. For example, a place you visited could be described as:

- isolated
- distant
- lonely
- private.

a   With a partner, discuss:

- What idea would your reader have about the place from each of these words?
- Do they all give the same impression?

b   Use the sentence below to experiment with using each word in turn. What effect does it have to exchange 'isolated' for one of the other words? Do all the sentences mean the same?

> The house was isolated as it was so far from the village.

Another type of vocabulary that can have a strong impact on the reader's understanding is **adverbs**. Adverbs are linked to *verbs*, and give information about *how* something is being done. The choice of adverb can also change the meaning of a sentence. For example:

The mother shouted angrily.

The mother shouted happily.

The mother shouted encouragingly.

Look at this simple sentence:

The man walked down the road.

It can be made more interesting by using adjectives and adverbs.

For example:

Adjectives ← The old man walked down the busy road hesitantly. ← Adverb

You could even change the verb: The old man shuffled slowly down the busy road.

Key terms

Adjective: describing words that tell you more about a noun – for example, the *tired* boy ran slowly.

Adverb: words that give details about how a verb is being done – for example, the boy ran *slowly*.

Noun: a word that denotes somebody or something. For example, the *boy* ran.

Activity

4

a Identify the adjectives and adverbs in the following sentences:

The young man briskly walked down the narrow road.
The miserable man walked gloomily down the dark road.
The successful man walked cheerily down the crowded road.

b In each of the above sentences, change the verb using a synonym of 'walked'.

c Using the two simple sentences below, experiment with adding adjectives and adverbs and changing the verb. Aim to have at least three different versions of each sentence.

A woman went into the shop.
My friend ate his lunch.

d Compare your sentences with another student. Decide which ones are the most effective.

Choosing words for effect

Writers influence their readers through their choice of words. They experiment with different words to get the effect they want.

Look at these three versions of the same piece of writing (Texts A, B and C). The writer has tried out different words to make each text have a different effect on the reader.

A

The old lady was dressed in a thick coat with flat shoes. She carried a handbag and an umbrella. Her eyes were blue and clear. Her hair was wispy and white, but it was mostly covered by a hat.

B

The old woman was dressed in a shabby brown coat with strange pointed boots. She carried a large holdall and a stick with a carved head on the handle. Her eyes were bloodshot and she wore glasses with thick 'jamjar' lenses. Her hair was wild and grey, but it was mostly covered by a black lace veil.

C

The elderly lady was dressed in a light summery coat with smart shoes. She carried a designer handbag and had a small dog on a lead. Her eyes were twinkling blue and she wore gold framed glasses. Her hair was carefully cut and styled, but it was mostly covered by an elegant hat.

Activities

5 With a partner, discuss:
- the different impressions created by each text
- which description is most likely to make the reader feel sorry for the old woman and why
- which one you think is the most effective and why.

6 **a** Choose the right words to help you:
- write four sentences which create a picture of a happy child
- write four sentences which create a picture of a sad child.

b Highlight the words you have used to create a picture of:
- a happy child
- a sad child.

Choosing vocabulary for audience and purpose

It is important to choose vocabulary that is suitable for your purpose and audience. Always make sure you know:

- what you are trying to achieve in your writing
- who you are writing for.

This will affect the words you choose. For example, you would choose simpler words if you were writing for young children than you would if you were writing for adults.

Read through the extracts below (Texts D and E); both texts have been written to inform. The annotations show you how the words have been chosen for different aged readers.

D

The Loch Ness Monster

People who live near Loch Ness think there might be a creature living in it which might be called a 'monster'. It has also been seen by holidaymakers and fishermen. They all describe something which is not an animal found in a zoo! It sounds more like a dinosaur! But, there are hardly any good photos of this creature which would help to prove if it is really there!

E

The Mystery of the Loch Ness Monster

Legend has it, that Loch Ness has been inhabited by mysterious creatures for hundreds of years and, though probably more like dinosaurs than anything currently alive, these have been referred to as 'monsters'. Recent advances in technology and science should have made it easier to identify and track any such creatures, but that has so far not proved to be the case! The numbers of reported sightings of the 'monster' increases yearly, but there is no definitive evidence for its existence – except for a few grainy black and white photos.

These are words that mean similar things. But note that the words are shorter and simpler to read in Text D.

Similar information but the language in Text E is more adult and gives more details.

Refers to something the reader would know about. In Text D it is zoos; in Text E it is progress in science.

Both texts have the same subject but the content and words are matched to the intended audience. Text D is written for children; Text E is written for adults.

7

a With a partner, read the two texts below (Texts F and G). Work out which is written for children and which is written for adults. List the words and phrases you could highlight to show why you think this.

F

Reported sightings of 'Bigfoot' exist across most of the globe, in any area which is remote, mountainous and heavily wooded. Also known as 'Yeti' or 'Sasquatch', the furry humanoid being leaves distinct traces of its existence in various ways. Most common are the enormous five-toed footprints left in mud or snow, but observers also report an eerie howling or strands of coarse reddish-brown hair caught on trees.

G

The 'Yeti' is the name given to a creature which is supposed to live in mountains and woods. People who claim to have seen these creatures can describe them well. It walks on its hind legs, like a man. It has brown or grey fur. It may make a weird howling sound. But the most common clue it leaves are its huge footprints in mud or snow.

b Choose an animal, real or legendary. Using the texts above as models, write two informative paragraphs. One should be written using words suitable for a child, the other using words suitable for an adult. Your paragraphs should contain about five sentences. Remember to:

- give information about your chosen animal
- choose your words to suit each audience.

c In each paragraph, highlight examples of words you have chosen to suit your child or adult audience.

Check your learning

Read the paragraphs below. They have been written by a student who has not really thought about how to make them interesting. He has also not written them for a specific audience.

> John went out for a walk. It was a nice morning, so he decided to visit the park.
>
> In the park, there were people doing different things; some were walking their dogs; some had brought their children; some were jogging and others, like him, were walking. An ice-cream van was parked near the lake. John bought an ice-cream and sat on a bench to eat it.
> He watched the ducks on the lake. There were some children sailing boats.
>
> John heard someone shout and when he looked a boy had fallen into the lake. He had been trying to get his boat out and fallen in. It did not look as if he could swim. John went to the water's edge. He jumped in and pulled out the boy. He had saved his life.

Your task is to make these paragraphs more interesting for a teenage reader. Write the story out again for this different audience. Remember to:

- look back over the chapter to remind yourself of the techniques you have practised
- think about which words could be changed or added to
- look at including more adjectives and adverbs
- choose different verbs that will make the text more interesting
- experiment with different words to create certain feelings in the reader.

Share your writing with another student and listen to their comments about what you have written. Make improvements to your writing and write a final draft.

Stretch yourself *k!*

Choose your favourite school subject. Write about it in a way that would be suitable for Year 7 students. Aim to:

- inform them about the subject
- make it more interesting
- use appropriate words suitable for Year 7 students.

17

Different sentences

Objectives

In this chapter you will:

experiment with sentences of different types

think about the effects that the sentence structures have on the reader.

Sentences

Spend a few minutes recapping what you remember a sentence is. If you are unsure, you could check by explaining to another student what you think a sentence is and what it is expected to have in it which makes it a sentence.

There are three main types of sentence.

Simple sentences

Simple sentences are just that … simple! Look at these examples:

> Jon screamed.
>
> The dog bit his leg.

They each have a subject and a verb.

Key terms

Simple sentence: at its most simple, contains one subject and one verb.

Activities

1 With a partner, identify the verb and the subject in each of the following simple sentences:

> The girl pushed the door. The door was heavy. She pushed harder. It swung open. She smiled. The sun was shining.

2

a Write six simple sentences of your own to continue this story. Highlight the subject and the verb in each of your sentences.

b Swap your sentences with a partner. Check that the subject and verb in each sentence is correctly highlighted.

c Discuss:
- when you would use simple sentences in your writing
- the problem with using too many simple sentences.

Compound sentences

Simple sentences are useful, but you wouldn't want to use them all the time. If you did, your writing would be quite boring.

Compound sentences use connectives to join two simple sentences together. Some examples of connectives include: and; but; then; and because.

For example:

Connective

> Jon screamed because the dog bit his leg.

If you took out the connective 'because', you would be left with two simple sentences:

> Jon screamed. The dog bit his leg.

Activity

3

a Look at the three compound sentences below. Identify the connective in each one.

> The girl pushed the door but it was heavy. She pushed harder and it swung open. She smiled because the sun was shining.

b Continue this story by writing three compound sentences. You could use connectives to join three of the simple sentences you wrote in Activity 2 as your starting point. Underline the connective you use in each compound sentence.

Complex sentences

In their simplest form, complex sentences use one main clause, which could be a sentence on its own. They then have one related point. This is contained in a **subordinate clause**. A subordinate clause does not make complete sense on its own.

> Though he had only tried to stroke it, the dog bit his leg.

Subordinate clause.

Main clause.

Key terms

Clause: a group of words that expresses an event or a situation. A sentence is made up of one or more clauses. A main clause is complete on its own and can form a complete sentence.

Subordinate clause: this is connected to the main clause and cannot exist on its own.

The subordinate clause can come after the main clause. For example:

The dog bit his leg, leaving a large red gash.

The subordinate clause can come in the middle of the main clause. For example:

The dog, though he had only tried to stroke it, bit his leg.

Activity

4

a Copy the following sentences. In each one, highlight and label the main clause in one colour and the subordinate clause in another colour.

> Having spent all morning trapped in the library, the girl pushed the door.
>
> The door, which was made of ancient oak, was heavy.
>
> She pushed harder, determined to escape.
>
> With an eerie creaking sound, it swung open.
>
> Looking out to the distant horizon, she smiled.
>
> The sun, in all its glory, was shining.

b Rewrite the following sentences by moving the subordinate clause to a different place. You should not need to add or take away any of the words in the sentence.

> Having spent all morning trapped in the library, the girl pushed the door.
>
> She pushed harder, determined to escape.
>
> The sun, in all its glory, was shining.

Using a range of sentence structures

Remind yourself of the use of:

- simple sentences:

> The girl pushed the door. The door was heavy. She pushed harder. It swung open. She smiled. The sun was shining.

- compound sentences:

> The girl pushed the door but it was heavy. She pushed harder and it swung open. She smiled because the sun was shining.

- complex sentences:

> Having spent all morning trapped in the library, the girl pushed the door. The door, which was made of ancient oak, was heavy. She pushed harder, determined to escape. With an eerie creaking sound, it swung open. Looking out to the distant horizon, she smiled. The sun, in all its glory, was shining.

If you use any single kind of sentence too much, it becomes boring to read.

The best kind of writing mixes simple, compound and complex sentences. Look at the mixture in the following:

> The girl, having spent all day inside the cold and dark library, pushed the door. It was heavy and would not move. With a determined effort, she pushed harder and it swung open, much to her surprise. With her first glimpse of the September day, she smiled. The sun was shining.

Simple sentence

Compound sentence

Complex sentence

It is important that you show you are able to use different sentence types when you write. Using different sentence structures makes your writing more interesting to read. It allows you to emphasise certain points or draw attention to particular bits of information.

Look at this example:

> Emma ran away from home on Sunday.

In this example, Emma is the subject of the sentence, followed by 'ran away' as the verb. By changing the word order and varying the vocabulary a little, the writer can emphasise different aspects.

Read these examples and think about how the different ways of writing the sentence affect the meaning.

> Sadly, Emma ran away from home on Sunday.
> Emma, having decided to run away, left home on Sunday.
> On Sunday of all days, Emma ran away from home.

Activity

5
a Read the examples above. What do you notice about the effect of moving the words around like this? When you read each one, where do you put the emphasis?

b Do the changes make the sentences mean different things? Try to explain your answer.

c With a partner, discuss what you could write next for each example. Can you use the same second sentence for each? If not, why do you think this is?

Varying openings of sentences

Sometimes writers choose to repeat the opening word in a sequence of sentences to emphasise a particular point. This can be a very successful technique when used well. However, too many sentences starting in the same way without good reason can result in a fairly repetitive and boring piece of writing.

Activities

6 Using the following sentence as your starting point, write three different sentences in which you emphasise different things:

> The sun was shining on Saturday.

Remember you can change the word order and vary the vocabulary.

> Writers experiment with different structures and vocabulary to try and achieve a particular effect on a reader. They use simple, compound or complex sentences at certain points to change the effect. When you write, make sure you have a mix of sentence structures.

7 **a** Look at the words listed below:

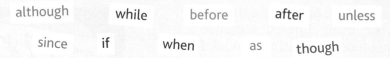

although   while   before   after   unless

since   if   when   as   though

These words are often used to make sentence openings interesting. Choose five of the words and use them to start your own complex sentences based on this simple sentence:

> John was late for the rehearsal.

b Compare your sentences with another student. Does your choice of opening word affect where the emphasis comes in the sentence? What effect does each sentence have on you when you read it?

8 Read Text A. Certain parts of the text have been highlighted. Match the annotations to the appropriate letter.

'This word is repeated to emphasise how many awful things the girl has experienced. It also helps the reader to understand that the girl had no choice in what she did.'

'A clear and straightforward simple sentence – it emphasises the purpose of the speaker.'

'A complex sentence which puts the emphasis on the number of children fighting and dying in wars and leaves the reader with that final thought.'

'This word is repeated to remind readers of the age of the 'soldiers'. It emphasises how young they are and is likely to make readers feel more sorry for them.'

'A compound sentence which links two closely connected details.'

'Uses adult vocabulary to emphasise the horror of the situation.'

Sentences in action

Now you are going to look at how a writer has used different sentence structures to draw attention to certain points.

Ⓐ

Ⓐ

Child soldiers

Ⓑ

'I would like you to give a message. Please do your best to tell the world what is happening to us, the children. So that other children don't have to pass through this violence.'

The 15-year-old girl who ended an interview to Amnesty International with this plea was forcibly abducted at night from her home by the Lord's Resistance Army (LRA), an armed opposition movement fighting the Ugandan Government. She was made to beat a boy who tried to escape. She saw another boy punished violently for not raising the alarm when a friend ran away. She was beaten when she dropped a water container and ran for cover under gunfire. She received 35 days of military training and was sent to fight the government army.

Ⓒ

Ⓓ

The use of children as soldiers has been universally condemned as abhorrent and unacceptable. Yet over the last ten years hundreds of thousands of children have fought and died in conflicts around the world.

Ⓔ

Ⓕ

www.child-soldiers.org

Check your learning

a With a partner, think about how the mother of a child soldier might feel. Discuss what she might feel about:
- her child being taken to be a soldier
- what may happen to the child next
- the conditions in which the child might be living
- hopes about the future.

b Record the ideas that you both have in a way that you will be able to use. This may be as a mind map, a list or in notes. You could also use some of the ideas in the article.

c With a partner, write the opening five sentences of an account from the mother's point of view. This could be to explain who she is and what has happened. You may wish to write it using first-person narrative.

d Using the rest of your ideas, continue to write an account on your own showing the mother's thoughts and feelings. Consider the following:
- Try to use a mix of simple, compound and complex sentences to create particular effects.
- Try to vary the ways that you start your sentences, to make the text more interesting for a reader.
- Ask another student or a member of staff to read your account. Ask them to pick out two things you have done well and make one suggestion for how it could be improved. You may also be asked to do this for another student.

18

Writing non-fiction

Non-fiction writing is based on real (or factual) events. It can provide information, but also entertain, advise, argue or persuade. To be successful in GCSE English or GCSE English Language, you will need to understand how to write non-fiction texts in an interesting and entertaining way.

Objectives

In this chapter you will:

learn how texts are structured

learn how to organise information into texts

learn how to write non-fiction texts.

'SCHAMA IS A GENIUS OF STORYTELLING...'
The Times

SIMON SCHAMA

THE

AMERICAN

FUTURE

A HISTORY
FROM THE FOUNDING FATHERS
TO BARACK OBAMA

twilight

STEPHENIE MEYER

Activity

1

a With a partner, read the list of types of writing below:

- newspaper article
- novel
- science report
- film review
- play, tourist brochure
- biography
- poem
- instructions.

- fairy story
- travel book
- magazine article
- medical record
- job description
- film script
- thriller

Which texts are fiction and which are non-fiction? Copy the Venn diagram below and use it to sort the texts. Texts that you think are a mixture of fiction and non-fiction should go in the overlapped section.

b Compare your ideas with another pair. Be prepared to defend your decisions and choices.

c What do you notice about the spread of texts in your Venn diagram? Discuss the reasons for this with the group.

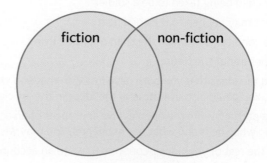

fiction   non-fiction

Newspaper articles

One of the most widely read non-fiction text types is newspapers. Many newspaper stories cover these five questions:

- Who?
- What?
- When?
- Where?
- How?

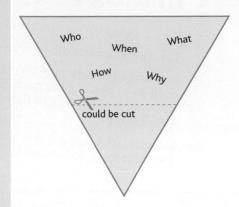

A journalist tries to give readers the answers to these questions in the first two or three paragraphs of their story. This is because some of the paragraphs at the end of the article may be cut to make room for another article. This is sometimes called the 'inverted pyramid' structure.

Read the sentences below (Text A). They contain all the information needed for a newspaper article. The text marking shows where the different questions are answered.

A mouse stole part of a leopard's lunch without being harmed by the leopard. It was in Santago Rare Leopard Project, yesterday. The scene was spotted by Casey Gutteridge, a 19-year-old student.

Who was involved.

What happened.

How the event resulted.

Where the event occurred.

When it took place.

A journalist needs to first 'hook' the readers and then give them the details in an interesting and entertaining way.

Although you are given all the information related to the story, it is not very interesting. It doesn't grab your attention.

Now read Text B, the actual newspaper article to see how the journalist did write it.

Ⓑ

In a Tight Spot! The Mouse that Roared

Here's a game of cat and mouse that didn't follow any of the usual rules.

This tiny thief was dicing with death when it helped itself to a leopard's lunch.

But instead of flattening the intruder with a huge paw, 12-year-old Sheena was nervous of it and tried to nudge it away with her nose – and the hungry mouse ignored her. The bizarre scene was captured by student Casey Gutteridge, 19, at the Santago Rare Leopard Project in Welwyn, Hertfordshire.

He said, 'The leopard was pretty surprised – she sniffed the mouse and flinched a bit. But the mouse just carried on eating.'

John Ingham, Environment Editor, *Daily Express*, 5 June 2009

Activities

2

a How does the headline make Text B sound interesting? Hint: look at the way the mouse is described!

b The first line of Text B doesn't give you answers to any of the five questions. How has the writer linked the headline with the first paragraph? Which words in the first paragraph has the writer chosen to make the event sound light-hearted and surprising?

c The writer has chosen his words carefully. Think about and explain the effect of the underlined phrases in this sentence.

> This <u>tiny thief</u> was <u>dicing with death</u> when it helped itself to a <u>leopard's lunch</u>.

d How is Text B more interesting than the factual account (Text A) that you read first? Explain your answer to another student and compare your ideas.

3

a Look at the picture of Verity below. Using the factual paragraph that follows, work with a partner to rewrite the account in a more interesting way. You also need a headline to go with the image.

> An orphaned baby hare has been bottle raised by Trudy Snell in Staithes, North Yorkshire. She found it on the grass verge last weekend, after its mother had been killed by a car. She has called the baby hare Verity.

b Share your story with another pair and discuss the following:
- Was the headline suitable?
- Do the words and phrases keep the reader interested?
- Have the five questions, Who?, What?, When? and How? been answered?

Organising ideas *k!*

Text C is a story about a Mako shark sighting in Cornwall. The writer has made sure the five questions are answered, but has also tried to link ideas throughout the story. She has varied the vocabulary to make sure the reader does not become bored and has provided new information in each paragraph which links with the ideas earlier on.

Activity

4

a Read Text C. You are going to track how the writer makes links within and between paragraphs. Copy and complete the following table:

Reference to the shark	References to the eye-witness	Details relating to time	Words chosen to show the danger of a Mako
A killer Mako (line 1)	Britain's top shark-hunter, Frank Vinnicombe, 86 (lines 2–3)	yesterday (line 3)	killer (line 1) tore (line 1)

C

A killer Mako shark leapt out of the sea and tore through a fisherman's catch – off Cornwall's coast. Britain's top shark-hunter Frank Vinnicombe, 86, told yesterday how the 13ft man-eater savaged his mackerel haul.

The angling legend – the last to catch a Mako here in 1980 – said: 'This was a beast, around 350–400lb. It jumped straight out of the water, which other sharks don't do, and tore my catch to shreds.'

'I've been fishing off the coast here every day of my life and I've seen more British sharks than anyone alive. This was a Mako.'

Shortfin Mako – known for attacking boats and swimmers – are the world's fastest sharks, reaching speeds of nearly 50mph. They have been reported in British waters in recent years. But grandad-of-eight Frank's eye-witness account is the first reliable testimony for decades.

Virginia Wheeler, 'Killer Shark in Angler Attack' *The Sun*, 5 June 2009

With a partner, recap on how it is necessary to make sure that what you write is clearly organised. This means that you need to think about the order in which you present your ideas. Using paragraphs helps your readers to follow your ideas more easily.

Remember, you should start a new paragraph whenever you change:

- the subject you are writing about
- the speaker
- the time.

Talk about when you might use long developed paragraphs and when you might use short ones.

Text C is a good example of 'tabloid paragraphing', using the short paragraphs often found in tabloid newspapers. It provides an easy way for readers to gather a lot of information quickly. However, tabloid paragraphing is not suitable for longer pieces of writing where a viewpoint or opinion is being developed.

In the exam or controlled assessment you might be asked to create a story based on a commission. You will be expected to:

- use developed paragraphs
- make links within and between paragraphs
- use different techniques to make your article interesting.

Activity

5

a   Use your knowledge about structure of non-fiction texts to plan and write a newspaper article. Use the basic story, quotes and facts below to help you.

Basic story:

Two walkers on Dartmoor have claimed they have seen a black panther. They saw it come out of woodland and run towards them before turning and going over a hill. This happened two days ago. They later came across the body of a sheep, which had clearly been killed and partly eaten.

Quotes you may want to use:

'I've seen panthers before – but only in a zoo!' (Kay Walters, aged 32)

'The sheep carcass had definitely been ripped apart. No dog could have done that.' (Kay Walters)

'When it came towards us, I thought we were going to be attacked. It was huge.' (Ben Matthews, aged 31)

'We would have stood no chance if it had got its claws into us!' (Ben Matthews)

Facts about panthers in the UK:

They used to live wild in the UK, but were hunted until they became extinct over 1,000 years ago.

Some people bought panther cubs as pets, but weren't able to look after them properly. They released them into the wild when they became adults.

An adult panther would need to kill a sheep-sized animal every other day to survive.

An adult panther can grow up to 2 metres in length and weigh up to 120kg.

Aim to write four paragraphs. The first one could cover:

- what the event was
- who was involved
- where they were
- when it happened.

Activity

6

Plan what you will include in each of the other paragraphs. Use Text C to give you some ideas. Think about:

- using varied words to keep the reader interested, for example different ways you could describe the panther
- linking the paragraphs by repeating names, or choosing verbs that mean similar things
- varying sentences by using simple, compound and complex ones

- using facts and quotes to make the story more dramatic.

Write around 150–200 words and don't forget to include a headline

b Share your article with another student and comment on each other's work.

Check your learning

a Newspapers and magazines often use topical issues to write an 'editorial'. Editorials seek to persuade the reader to agree with the writer's opinion. Read Text D and the annotations to see how the writer does this.

D

Pets are a health risk!

Why do parents think that letting their kids have a pet is a good idea?

Yet again this week, we hear about another toddler being attacked by the family pet. Luckily, the baby did not die – but she will be scarred for the rest of her life. And by an animal she loved and the family trusted!

In my own family, our pets have caused much heartache and upset for us all. It's very hard to explain to a crying six year old, why our much loved dog had not come home from the vet's, or that his hamster had escaped or when he might see his wandering kitten again.

I keep saying 'No more pets,' and mean it at the time. I know my son and his mother love animals, but I don't think we need to have them living with us. The emotional cost is just too high. I don't believe a child needs to 'get used' to coping with loss like this when he's so young. There will be enough time as he gets older to accept that life is harsh and nothing lives forever.

Next time, I'm going to try and stay strong, and resist their pleas for whatever animal they fancy. It is for their emotional health after all!

Snappy dramatic opening to engage reader and introduce subject.

Recent example to back up opening question.

Includes personal experiences and examples to support writer's ideas. Uses personal pronouns ('we' and 'our') and words such as 'loved' to make this emotive.

Long complex sentence listing family's experiences. It draws attention to the crying child by putting that first.

Develops personal views and includes writer's opinion. Repeats 'I' to emphasise the personal nature of what is said.

Sums up the writer's views and finishes with a short sentence for emphasis.

b Using Text D as a model, write a five-paragraph editorial about a topic you feel strongly about. Aim to make your reader agree with your views. Organise your writing and choose your words and sentence structures carefully to have maximum impact.

c Ask another student to comment on the effectiveness of your writing.

19

Writing fiction

Objectives

In this chapter you will:

learn more about how texts are structured

learn how to organise creative ideas into texts

learn how to write in different fiction formats.

You are going to experiment with three different forms of creative writing and look at the differences between them. You will eventually choose one form in which to write, using the notes you have made as you work through this chapter.

Planning to be creative

Many people make up and tell stories even when they are very young. They might make up stories about dolls or action figures or tell stories to younger brothers and sisters. To do this, they use their imagination and match their story to the person they are telling it to.

Activity

1

a With a partner, share memories of stories you have told, or remember being told when you were younger. Here are some questions to help jog your memory:

- Did you have a favourite story/film/book?
- What do you remember about the details?
- Did any stories you read/heard/saw make you feel a particular way?

b When do you still tell/read/watch made-up stories? Do you prefer to read, listen to, watch or tell them?

Choosing what you know

Often the best way to start a piece of creative writing is to begin with something based on personal experience.

Activity

2

Think back to an event in your childhood that you can remember clearly. It might be an incident at school, a birthday present or something dramatic that you did not really understand. Jot down the things that you can recall connected with it – for example:

- Where were you?
- When did it happen?
- Who were you with?
- What were you wearing?
- What smells and sounds do you recall?
- How did you feel?
- What happened?

You will add to these notes in a later activity.

Writing script

Drama texts and plays are made up of dialogue and written as a script.

A script is written to be heard (radio plays) or acted (films, TV programmes or stage plays). The audience would not normally read the text. The actors who perform it use their voices and body language to help the audience understand the events that occur and the characters' emotions.

Read Text A, an extract from the script of the play *Blood Brothers* by Willy Russell. It is taken from early in the play where two boys meet for the first time by accident. They do not realise it but they are actually non-identical twins who have been separated as babies.

The features of a script are annotated for you.

Key terms

Drama: a play written to be acted on a stage or made into a TV or film production.

(A)

Mickey: I'm older than you. I'm nearly eight.

Edward: Well, I'm nearly eight, really.

Mickey: What's your birthday?

Edward: July the eighteenth.

Mickey: So is mine.

Edward: Is it really?

Mickey: Ey, we were born on the same day … that means we can be blood brothers. Do you wanna be my blood brother, Eddie?

Edward: Yes, please.

Mickey (producing a penknife): It hurts y'know. (He puts a nick in his hand) Now, give us yours.

MICKEY nicks EDWARD'S hand, then they clamp hands together.

See, that means that we're blood brothers an' that we always have to stand by each other…

Mrs Johnstone: Mickey … Mickey …

Edward: Is that your mummy?

Mickey: Mam … Mam, this is my brother.

Willy Russell, *Blood Brothers,* Methuen Drama, 1983

The name of the character who is speaking is followed by a colon (:) and then the words they speak. A new line is started each time a new character speaks.

Stage directions. These are instructions for the actor playing the part. They can also be used to describe the scenery or setting.

These are the words spoken by the character. Notice that speech marks are not used in script.

3

a How does the writer show that the characters are children? Think about:

- what they say
- what they do.

b How does the writer show differences between the characters through the words they use? What can you work out about Mickey and Edward from the way they speak?

c Do you think the scene is **realistic**? Give reasons for your answer.

4

a With a partner, discuss what else the boys might talk about once Mrs Johnstone has left. Write ten lines of script in which both characters talk and find out more about each other. Use similar dialogue to that used by the writer, so that the characters stay the same.

b Swap your script with another pair. Read the lines aloud as though you were actors. Have the writers used similar speech styles to those in the extract?

Writing prose

Prose is the form of writing used in **novels** and **short stories**. These are read, not seen. Unlike a script writer, prose writers need to describe the setting, what is happening, and the appearance, thoughts and feelings of the characters. Much prose is written from a single viewpoint. This is sometimes in the form of **first-person narrative**.

Read Text B, *When the Wasps Drowned* by Clare Wigfall. The extract comes half way through the story while the narrator is looking after her younger sister in the summer holidays. Notice that the paragraphs are of different lengths and contain a mixture of description, dialogue and narrative.

Some of the features are annotated for you.

Key terms

Realistic: similar to events or speech in real life.

Prose: the usual way that writing or speech is recorded; not poetry or drama.

Novel: a long piece of writing in prose; usually a fiction story.

Short story: a shorter piece of writing in prose; often with a 'twist' at the end.

First-person narrative: writing from the single point of view of a narrator using 'I', 'me', 'my', 'we' and 'our'. This gives the reader only one opinion of what is happening and lets them know the thoughts and feelings of the narrator.

B

When the Wasps Drowned

It was the glint that caught my eye. I only saw it as she jerked her hand at the buzz of a fly. Wedged on her thumb was a thin gold ring, studded with small diamonds. There was dirt lodged between the stones, but still they caught the sunlight and glimmered. At first I didn't react. I just lay there watching.

'Therese,' I questioned finally, 'where did you get that ring?'

'Found it', she sighed.

I heaved myself up by one elbow and took her hand in mine to look more closely at the small piece of jewellery. 'Where?' I asked.

Therese yawned before rolling onto one side and up. She walked me to the hole they'd been digging. It was deep and long now, tunnelling under our wall and into Mr Moredcai's garden. We knelt down and peered into its depths. It was too dark to see much. Therese took my hand and guided it into the hole. I knew straight away what it was I could feel but I told Therese to run in and find the torch. She came back a moment later and we angled the light. At the end of the tunnel a pale hand reached towards us.

Clare Wigfall, *When the Wasps Drowned*

The writer has used first-person narrative. Notice how the reader discovers everything through the narrator's eyes.

The spoken words are enclosed by speech marks. Verbs are used to give the reader clues as to how the words are spoken.

Description is used to create a picture for the reader of what is happening and what can be seen.

The narrator builds suspense. She does not 'tell' the reader that there is a body buried in the garden next door. She lets the reader work it out by giving a series of clues.

Activities

5
a How does the writer show that Therese is a child?

b How does the writer show that the narrator is older than Therese?

c How does the writer use description to help the reader picture the ring?

d How does the writer create tension in the final paragraph?

e Why do you think the writer chose to use first-person narrative in this story?

6
a Think about how you could continue this story. Write two more paragraphs, using the first person, in which you describe and build the tension further.

b Compare your paragraphs with another student's. Which do you think are the most effective and why?

Writing poetry

Writers can choose to write poetry to show emotions, situations and ideas in a 'capsule' form. Some poems can be likened to a 'snapshot' – a photo that captures just a single moment or event in time. Poems can 'capture' things in the same way, but use words instead of a picture.

Poems are usually shorter than scripts and prose. However, they are written in a condensed form and can contain many different images. Words are chosen carefully to have maximum impact on the reader.

Read Text C below, *Brendon Gallacher* by Jackie Kay, which also appears in the AQA Anthology. The poet is writing about a childhood friend. Some of the features have been annotated for you.

Brendon Gallacher

He was seven and I was six, my Brendon Gallacher.
He was Irish and I was Scottish, my Brendon Gallacher.
His father was in prison; he was a cat burglar.
My father was a communist party full-time worker.
He had six brothers, I had one, my Brendon Gallacher.

He would hold my hand and take me by the river
where we'd talk all about his family being poor.
He'd get his mum out of Glasgow when he got older.
A wee holida some place nice. Some place far.
I'd tell my mum all about my Brendon Gallacher

how his mum drank and his daddy was a cat burglar.
And she'd say, 'Why not have him round to dinner?'
No. No I'd say, he's got big holes in his trousers.
I like meeting him by the burn in the open air.
Then one day after we'd been friends for two years,

One day when it was pouring and I was indoors,
My mum says to me, 'I was talking to Mrs Moir
who lives next door to your Brendon Gallacher.
Didn't you say his address was 24 Novar?
She says there are no Gallachers at 24 Novar'

There never have been any Gallachers next door.'
And he died then, my Brendon Gallacher,
flat out on my bedroom floor, his spiky hair,
his impish grin, his funny, flapping ear.
Oh Brendon, Oh my Brendon Gallacher.

Jackie Kay, 'Brendon Gallagher'

The writer has used first-person narrative view. This helps the reader to understand and identify with the poet's feelings and memories.

The poet repeats this phrase six times. The word 'my' suggests that the boy is special to her.

The poet gives details about Brendon's appearance, life and family to convince has mother (and the reader) that he does exist.

There is dialogue between the poet and her mother but only the mother's words are enclosed in speech marks. This makes the poet's answers seem more like thoughts.

Activities

7

a Read through Text C with another student and identify the details that the writer uses to:
  - make the boy seem real
  - show the girl's feelings for the boy.

b At what point in the poem do you realise that Brendon is a made-up friend?

c Many children have an imaginary friend. Write the first verse of a poem in which you start to describe an imaginary friend. Write in the first person. Aim to make the friend seem real.

8 Work through the following steps:

Step 1: The first thing you need to do is to choose your task carefully. Read the following three tasks. Think carefully about each one and take note of the warnings. Choose one task from the following three creative writing questions.

a The controlled assessment might ask you to use a text as a basis for your writing, but to change the form. The poem (Text C) is about an imaginary friend. Use this poem as the starting point for a piece of writing on the same topic. Choose which form you think would best allow you to show your ideas and creative writing skills.

Warning: If you choose a, you cannot write a poem. You can write a script or a story.

b The controlled assessment task might ask you to write creatively in response to an opening that is provided for you. Use the following opening sentences to write a short story in first-person narrative:

> My spade hit something. I knew digging here had been the right thing to do …

Warning: If you choose b, you must write a story.

c Go back to the notes you made in Activity 2, about an event in your childhood. Use these as your starting point to write a script, a story or a series of poems about memories of childhood.

Warning: if you choose poetry in c, you must write more than one poem.

Step 2: Plan your ideas carefully. Think about situations, settings and characters and how best to show these. Decide on the order in which you will write.

Step 3: Spend an hour writing. Read through what you have written every ten minutes.

Writing for yourself

For your controlled assessment you will be asked to write creatively using script, prose or poetry. Whichever you choose, you will need to show that you can use features of the form you have chosen. Look back through this chapter before doing Activity 8.

Check your learning

Swap your writing with another student. Use the following questions to help you assess the writing.

Has the writer:
- focused on the task
- taken note of the warnings and chosen an allowed form
- set out and organised the writing in a way that is suitable for the chosen form
- used language well to create an impression of situations, settings and characters
- written something that you enjoyed reading?

Once you have thought about these questions, tell the writer what you liked about their writing and offer advice on anything you think could be improved.

20

Adapting forms

In this chapter you will look at how a writer's intended audience and purpose can change the way a text is written, even when the subject of the text is the same. The way a text is written is called the form. Different forms include: letters, novels, adverts, web pages, newspapers, etc. Work through the Review and reflect on audience and purpose to refresh you memory before working through the chapter.

Objectives

In this chapter you will:

learn more about how writers adapt their writing to suit purpose and audience

think about how form affects writing

experiment with language to create different texts

ensure your writing suits your purpose and audience.

Review and reflect

Try this quick quiz to make quite sure you understand audience and purpose. There is only one correct answer for each question. Write down the letter of the one you think is correct.

1 The purpose of a text is:

   a the section in a text that deals with a particular topic

   b the reason a text has been written

   c the type of text it is, for example, a letter.

2 The intended audience of a text is:

   a the people who the writer thinks will hear and/or read it

   b people who do not often read

   c people who listen to the radio.

3 The purpose of a magazine advertisement is usually:

   a to sell something

   b to give instructions

   c to explain rules.

4 The audience for a travel guide is probably:

   a people who have no interest in travel

   b children who want to build models

   c readers who want to visit that place.

5 Knowing the purpose and audience for a text helps the writer:

   a choose the right sort of language

   b use a suitable style of writing

   c both of the above.

Now compare your answers with those of another student and discuss anything you were uncertain about. Try to agree on which answer is the correct one.

Understanding audience and purpose of non-fiction writing

You have come across examples of non-fiction texts in other chapters. Now you are going to look at some examples of non-fiction texts written for different purposes and audiences.

Texts A and C are about the same place. They include some of the same details, but have different purposes and intended audiences. The form of each text is different and this has affected the words each writer has chosen and the sentence structures used.

Read Text A, which is taken from the website of Harewood House. Its purpose is to encourage families to visit. The annotations explain the main features of the writing.

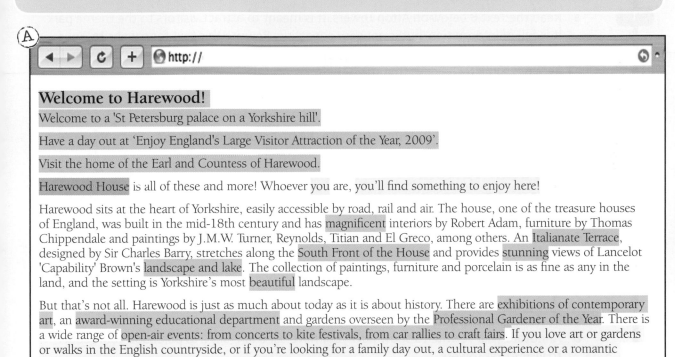

(A)

http://

Welcome to Harewood!

Welcome to a 'St Petersburg palace on a Yorkshire hill'.

Have a day out at 'Enjoy England's Large Visitor Attraction of the Year, 2009'.

Visit the home of the Earl and Countess of Harewood.

Harewood House is all of these and more! Whoever you are, you'll find something to enjoy here!

Harewood sits at the heart of Yorkshire, easily accessible by road, rail and air. The house, one of the treasure houses of England, was built in the mid-18th century and has magnificent interiors by Robert Adam, furniture by Thomas Chippendale and paintings by J.M.W. Turner, Reynolds, Titian and El Greco, among others. An Italianate Terrace, designed by Sir Charles Barry, stretches along the South Front of the House and provides stunning views of Lancelot 'Capability' Brown's landscape and lake. The collection of paintings, furniture and porcelain is as fine as any in the land, and the setting is Yorkshire's most beautiful landscape.

But that's not all. Harewood is just as much about today as it is about history. There are exhibitions of contemporary art, an award-winning educational department and gardens overseen by the Professional Gardener of the Year. There is a wide range of open-air events: from concerts to kite festivals, from car rallies to craft fairs. If you love art or gardens or walks in the English countryside, or if you're looking for a family day out, a cultural experience or a romantic afternoon, come to Harewood. We think you'll be delighted!

The short sentences give essential information. The writer puts these at the end so that the reader will remember the details.

The writer has chosen words and phrases that encourage people to visit the house and suggest they will enjoy it. The use of 'you' makes it sound as if the writer is speaking directly to the reader.

Adjectives are used to make the place sound attractive and interesting.

Different places are named to draw attention to the range of things the visitor can do there.

Hyperlinks indicate that there is more to know about Harewood House than there is space to mention on this page.

Non-fiction websites

The writer of Text A has tried to make the description appeal to a wide range of people. It is made to sound more personal by using pronouns like 'our' and 'you'. The focus is clearly on persuading the reader that this would be an enjoyable and interesting place for the family to visit.

Activity

1

a Read the Text B below on Alton Towers. It is meant to attract visitors to the theme park. It is full of information, but is not very appealing. Rewrite this text for a website. Your aim is to make it more appealing to families. You can change it in any way you wish, but here are some techniques that might help:

- Use adjectives that make it sound exciting.
- Address the reader directly to make it more personal.
- Vary the sentence structures to make the text more interesting.

B

Alton Towers

Alton Towers dates from the 8th century though the theme park was not built until the 20th century.

The theme park has plenty of big rides. These include Oblivion, Nemesis and Ripsaw. There are also rides for young children which are not as scary. There is a new water park which is open all year round. It has slides, bubble pools and flumes to play in.

b Annotate your rewrite to show how your have used language to persuade your reader to visit Alton Towers.

Non-fiction travel guides

Now read Text C, which also focuses on Harewood House but is taken from a travel guide to the whole of Britain. The purpose is to inform tourists about places of importance around the country. The writer was commissioned to write 50 words about each place. The annotations explain the main features of the writing.

Harewood House

Regal 18th century house built by John Carr with Woodland Garden, Bird Garden, Penguin Pond, and Paradise Garden with tropical wildlife. Robert Adam designed interiors and Thomas Chippendale made furniture. Spanish Library has Yorkshire landscapes by Turner. Gallery has 76ft long Adam ceiling with paintings of gods and goddesses.

J. Palmer (ed.) *Reader's Digest Touring Guide to Britain 1994*, The Reader's Digest Association Limited, 1994

The writer has used names of famous people connected with Harewood House. These are intended to interest adults who know of these people. They also help to suggest it is a place of importance.

The writer uses only factual details to inform the reader. All these are things that can be seen there, but the writer has not tried to make them attractive to visitors.

The whole text is only four sentences. They contain details about the house and what can be seen there. The writer does not address the reader directly and adopts a formal tone. Though the writer of Text B is describing the same place as Text A, the text is very different. It informs but does not aim to persuade the reader. The writer was limited to 50 words and had to carefully select which details to include.

In your own writing you will sometimes need to select which details to include and which to leave out. For example, if you write a section of your autobiography, you may choose to leave out some of the details about things that were not important, to concentrate on the events that did matter. This choice may be affected by your purpose and audience.

Activity (k!)

2

a With a partner, read the following facts about Buckingham Palace:

Official residence of the Queen.	Built in 1703.
In City of Westminster, London.	Smaller rooms decorated in Chinese regency style.
First called Buckingham House.	Garden is largest private one in London.
Contains works of art in the Royal Collection.	Garden parties are held in the summer
Extended by John Nash and Edward Blore in 19th century.	State rooms open to public in August and September.

b Together, you are going to write a short information text (no more than 60 words) about Buckingham Palace. Select five facts to use in your writing.

c Name the place and inform your reader about it. Use a writing style similar to the one used in Text B.

d Check your word count. If you have written more than 60 words, decide what to leave out and make cuts to your writing.

The final text (Text D) is taken from a website. It targets a different audience to the previous texts. Read the opening page from the 'Go Ape' website. Each paragraph gives different information to the reader. Read the text and the annotations that explain the main features of the writing.

The undisputed king of the jungle is Go Ape

Thanks for visiting our website. It's been lashed together with wire and ropes to tell you all about Go Ape – who we are, what we're up to this summer, and why we believe in the supernatural powers of bananas.

We've opened five courses in time for summer, which means new *Go Ape experiences* to try. No two courses are the same, but wherever you Go Ape you'll come face to face with a monkey*.

So gather your tribe and come and join us. Perhaps it's your birthday. Or you need to organise a corporate team day. Or maybe you just want to make like Tarzan and *swing through the trees* shouting, 'arrrh-a-arrrh-a-arrrhhhh!' We're fine with that too.

Don't forget, you can book online or over the phone, and if you want to treat your favourite monkey to some tree time, you can get gift vouchers here.

See you in the trees!

The Go Ape Tribe

*Actually, that's not strictly true. You'll get up close and personal with your inner monkey, but the legal people would like us to say you're unlikely to meet an actual monkey.

www.goape.co.uk

The writer has used a lot of personal pronouns to make the reader feel more involved and appeal to them directly. It sounds like the writer is almost talking to the reader personally.

The use of humour suggests that the place is fun to visit. Jokes about monkeys and Tarzan fit in with the name of the place.

The connectives offer the reader different reasons for visiting the place.

A positive quote from a well-known newspaper reinforces the impression that this is a good place to visit.

Italics in the main text are used to draw attention to certain phrases that emphasise that this experience takes place above ground.

Text D is not written for visitors in general. It targets people who want to have a bit of an adventure. It doesn't give the same amount of detail about the attraction as the other texts, but relies on making the activity sound fun and different. The writer will expect an interested reader to visit the other web pages, so does not need to put all the details on this page.

Activity k!

3   **a**   Look at Photo E. It is taken from the advertising material for a new indoor climbing trail. It is aimed at young people who want a new challenge and a taste of adventure. Write the opening web page for the new attraction. You are trying to encourage young people to try out what is on offer. Aim to write about five short paragraphs.

Make sure you:

- choose a suitable name for the attraction
- give reasons why this would be good to do
- use personal pronouns
- choose words that make it sound fun and exciting
- provide some information about what can be done there
- use a range of sentence structures and punctuation.

b   Swap your writing with another student. Check that their writing appeals to young people and includes the suggestions in the bullet points. Think about whether their text would encourage you to visit the place and share your response with them.

Check your learning

Write a commentary on the text you produced in Activity 3. In your commentary, explain:

- what the task was
- what your purpose and audience was
- the things you needed to think about before you started to write
- the techniques you used in order to achieve your purpose
- the techniques you used in order to target your audience
- how successful you think you were and your reasons for this.

21

Genres

What is 'genre'?

The French word '**genre**' means 'a kind or style, especially in art or literature'. You may have heard of some genres in music or film – for example:

Music:
- pop
- rock
- hip-hop
- classical.

Film:
- horror
- science fiction
- comedy
- action.

Objectives

In this chapter you will:

learn how to identify different genres

prepare to use your ideas to complete a longer writing task.

Activity

1

a With a partner, what other music and film genres can you think of? Try to add at least four to each list.

b Compare your list with another pair and share your ideas. How many different genres have you thought of?

When music or films belong to the same genre, it means that they will be similar to one another in some way – perhaps they are the same type of music or film, or they share the same sorts of features.

Text genres

Just as there are genres of music and films, there are also genres in writing. It is possible to spot features in texts that show you which genre a text belongs to.

- Some features might be linked to the **plot**, for example a story about a character who investigates murders could be part of the detective story genre.

- Sometimes the language shows the genre, for example horror stories might contain references to darkness, with gruesome details and terrifying sounds.

- Sometimes it is the setting which gives the reader clues about the genre.

Key terms

Genre: the style of something. In writing, this could be crime, horror, etc.

Plot: what the story is about, the storyline.

Identify genre

The setting is the place where events take place. The way that a setting is described can help the reader to understand how the characters feel there. As a reader, sometimes just reading about the place can also make you feel the same way. If a character is scared by being in a certain place, the reader can be too!

Read Texts A–C and think about the description of the places.

 A

The Martian desert was almost flat, flat and bare. Not even a scrub of vegetation existed here. This particular area had been dead and deserted for who knows how many thousands or millions of years. … It was getting cold. Even at Martian summer, he guessed the temperature to be barely above freezing. He could look directly at the sun in the sky. It was a dwarfed sun in a purple sky in which he could make out three or four stars.

Isaac Asimov, *Space Ranger*, New English Library, 1980

 B

Perched on a hill-top among olive trees, the new villa, white as snow, had a broad veranda running along one side, which was hung with a thick pelmet of grape–vine. In front of the house was a pocket handkerchief-sized garden, neatly walled, which was a solid tangle of wild flowers. The whole garden was overshadowed by a large magnolia tree, the glossy dark green leaves of which cast a deep shadow. … We had liked the villa the moment Spiro had shown it to us.

Gerald Durrell, *My Family and Other Animals*, Penguin, 1976

Background

Veranda: a type of porch that runs along the outside of a building.

Pelmet: a narrow covering that usually goes over the top of a window.

C

I hear her restless in the night, walking the floor, pacing up and down. I don't move in my bed, pretending I'm asleep. I know what she wants to do. I know that she wants to call him. I hope she doesn't. But I also know that Hallowe'en is coming and she must call. … Last night she went through the routine again. Pacing up and down, standing at the window looking out, then beside my bed.

Robert Cormier, *In the Middle of the Night*, Collins, 1995

Activities

2   **a**   Which genre do you think Text A belongs to?

      b   Pick out three details the writer has used that show you the setting is not on earth.

      c   What effect does the description of the sun and sky have on the reader?

3   **a**   Do you think Text B belongs to the same genre as Text A? Give reasons for your answer.

      b   What effect does the mention of so many plants and trees have on the reader?

      c   Rewrite the opening sentence of Text B to make it seem more like the opening of a horror story. Replace the words and phrases that have been underlined with ones that give a scarier atmosphere. For example, 'Perched' might be swapped for 'Hanging' or 'Alone'.

      d   Swap your work with a partner and decide who has created the most scary atmosphere.

4   **a**   Text C is from a novel. Which genre do you think it belongs to? Give reasons for your answer.

      b   How do you know the extract is not from an autobiography?

      c   How does the writer make the narrator sound worried?

5   **a**   Texts A, B and C come from different genres. One is from a thriller, another is from science-fiction and another is from an autobiography. Can you explain which is which?

      b   Choose either Text A or Text C and write a paragraph which could follow on from it. Aim to write in the same style as the author.

The next two texts are from different genres and are intended to:

- give the reader a clear image of what is being described
- convey a particular feeling about a scene.

Text D is from a science-fiction novel set in the future. The description is an account of the narrator's first visit to a city. Read Text D and the annotations.

Both Texts D and E are intended to give the reader a clear image of what is being described, but also convey a particular feeling about the scene.

D

Derelict houses, some burned out. Cracks in the road with weeds poking through. Piles of brick and glass and cement everywhere, all smashed up. It was hard to imagine what it must have been like in the old days, with cars and crowds and big stores and a million lights, like cities you see in ancient movies. Gran says she remembers cities that way, but it's hard to imagine … As we drove further in we passed a so-called residential development – multi-storey apartment blocks scattered across a wilderness of long grass and overgrown pathways. Most of the blocks were doorless and glassless and there was rubbish everywhere. Cans and bottles, plastic bags, filthy mattresses, the skeletons of baby buggies, you name it.

Robert Swindells, *Daz4Zoe*, Puffin, 1990

Groups of objects. These make the reader imagine what is being described. These groups describe different times, but the same place, so the contrast is quite shocking.

Adjectives are used effectively to draw attention to how little care is taken of the place.

The verbs suggest bad things have happened and sound almost violent.

The narrator repeats the same words to show the reader how shocked she is at what she can see. It makes the point very strongly that she has never seen anything like it before.

Activity

6 Now read Text E, taken from a supernatural thriller. Using the annotations for Text D as an example, decide how the writer has made the description of the boy's encounter with a strange fox sound threatening. Aim to identify three aspects of the writing that add to the tension.

E

The air seemed suddenly colder, and across the fields, all around him, he could see creeping in a low ground mist that he had not noticed before. Slowly it came pouring over the fences, relentless, like some huge crawling creature. From every direction it came, from the mountain, the valley, the lower slopes and when Will looked back at the grey fox standing stiff-legged in the field, he saw something else that gave a chill of terror to the mist. The fox was changing colour. With every moment, as he watched, its sleek body and bushy tail grew darker and darker, until it became almost black.

Susan Cooper, *The Grey King*, Bodley Head, 1984

7 Look at Photograph F. With a partner, you are going to write two short paragraphs using the photograph as a starting point. Your task is to make the two paragraphs as different as possible, so that you show two very different atmospheres in your writing.

F

a Paragraph 1: Imagine you have been on holiday to this place and really enjoyed your stay. Write a short description of the house and surroundings, which gives the reader the impression of how pleasant you found it and how much you liked your holiday.

b Paragraph 2: You are going to use the photograph as the basis for writing a description that is tense and threatening. Choose words that give the reader an impression of being scared and spooked by the house and mountains.

c Compare your descriptions with those of another pair. How successful has their word choice been? Do you respond to what they have written in the way they expect?

Changing form

The texts you have read so far have all been prose. Dramas (plays) can also be grouped according to genre. Dramas rely on dialogue to create the atmosphere and influence the feelings of the audience. A drama as spooky or tense as a ghost story, or as mysterious and puzzling as a detective novel.

Read Text G, an extract from the play *An Inspector Calls*. It is a play that seems to be about the suicide of a young woman. In this scene, a police inspector calls at the home of a family who might be involved.

G

Inspector:	(*impressively*) I'm a police inspector, Miss Birling. This afternoon a young woman drank some disinfectant and died, after several hours of agony, tonight in the Infirmary.
Sheila:	Oh – how horrible! Was it an accident?
Inspector:	No. She wanted to end her life. She felt she couldn't go on any longer.
Birling:	Well. Don't tell me that's because I discharged her from my employment nearly two years ago.
Eric:	That might have started it.
Sheila:	Did you Dad?
Birling:	Yes. The girl had been causing trouble in the works. I was quite justified.
Gerald:	Yes. I think you were. I know we'd have done the same thing. Don't look like that Sheila.
Sheila:	(*rather distressed*) Sorry! It's just that I can't help thinking about this girl – destroying herself so horribly – and I've been so happy tonight. Oh I wish you hadn't told me. What was she like? Quite young?
Inspector:	Yes. Twenty-four.
Sheila:	Pretty?
Inspector:	She wasn't pretty when I saw her today, but she had been pretty – very pretty.

J. B. Priestley, *An Inspector Calls*

Activity

8

a   Experiment with changing the form of Text G, from script to prose. It is a detective story – the inspector is trying to find out who is responsible for the young woman killing herself.

Rewrite this short scene as if you were either the Inspector or Sheila. Write in the first person explaining what happened, how you felt and what you were thinking. You can make up extra details if you want to.

Remember to:

● choose your words to suit the detective story genre

● build up a sense of tension and shock to influence the reader.

b   Swap your writing with another student's. Read their text and share your response to what they have written. Have they written as the Inspector or Sheila? Is the language suitable for the genre?

Developing ideas

For your GCSE English or English Language, you will need to use your knowledge about genres to write creatively.

In your exam or controlled assessment, you will need to write in a genre that you are familiar and confident with. This will improve your opportunities of getting a good mark.

Activity

9

'Looking from the top of the hill, he saw a sight that was completely unexpected.'

a   Use the above line as the opening sentence of a short story of about five to six paragraphs. Choose from either the science-fiction, thriller or detective genre. Plan your ideas before starting to write. Think about the following:

● which genre you will use

● who your character(s) will be

● what events you could include

● how you could move the story on from the opening sentence

● how you could describe your setting

● how you could use dialogue to keep the story moving and add to the atmosphere.

b   Share your story with a partner and discuss how well you think your partner managed to fit their story to the genre they chose.

Check your learning

a   Choose one genre of writing that you have looked at in this chapter and challenge another student to name two features found in that type of writing. Evaluate their responses against the work you have done.

b   To challenge each other further, pick a genre you have not looked at in this chapter. Each name a feature you think would be found in that genre. Discuss whether or not you agree with each other's ideas and, if not, explain why.

22 Making your writing skills count in the exam

Objectives

In this chapter you will:

learn more about how your writing is tested in the exam

study questions in a sample paper

plan, write and assess an answer

read other students' answers and the examiner's comments on them.

About the exam

In the study of the past nine chapters, you have been developing your skills in writing. These skills will help you to cope with the demands of the exam.

There is one exam paper in English and English Language. Its focus is:

- understanding and producing non-fiction texts.

The paper is divided into two sections:

- **Section A**: Reading (one hour) and worth 20 per cent of your final marks.
- **Section B**: Writing (one hour) and worth 20 per cent of your final marks.

There will be two writing tasks. You will be expected to do both of them. They may be linked by theme. You should aim to spend about 20 minutes on the shorter task and 40 minutes on the longer task. This includes planning and checking time.

Assessment Objectives

The Assessment Objectives are very important because they are the aims of your GCSE course. The examiners will be looking for how well you can fulfil these objectives in your exam. The Assessment Objectives are written for teachers to help them teach you the skills you need over the length of your course. It is, however, possible to break them down into more student-friendly language.

You have one hour in which to show the examiner the writing skills summarised in the Assessment Objectives. They are printed on the top of page 145. The annotations explain what you have to do.

Planning in the exam

Planning your answers could help you write better answers. A plan will give your answer a definite structure and will remind you of the points you want and need to include in your answer. Any plan should be brief, but useful. Avoid writing a long plan as you will only have one hour in the exam. Your plan could use one of the following methods:

- A list of topics you wish to include in your response.
- A mind map with linked points.
- A spidergram with sequenced ideas.

Aim to be clear, relevant and interesting

Think about what you have been asked to write. Make sure you know the features of the different forms and that you write in a way that fits the form

Remember your purpose

Write clearly, effectively and imaginatively, using and adapting forms and selecting vocabulary appropriate to task and purpose in ways which engage the reader.

Show that you have used a varied vocabulary range

Remember your audience – you want to make the reader read on with interest

Make sure your writing is organised into paragraphs and that you link the paragraphs by using connectives and related ideas. Plan in advance so that your ideas are well organised

Organise information and ideas into structured and sequenced sentences, paragraphs and whole texts, using a variety of linguistic and structural features to support cohesion and overall coherence.

Use headings and subheadings effectively and consistently

Use a mixture of simple, compound and complex sentences

Use effectively a range of sentence structures for clarity, purpose and effect, with accurate punctuation and spelling.

Use a range of punctuation accurately, with spelling that is mostly correct

How you can prepare for the exam

Students sometimes feel that it is difficult to revise for English or English Language exams. This is because of the wide range of questions that can be asked; students are not sure what topics may be covered. However, it is possible – and useful – to revise for the exam.

You probably know which areas in the exam most bother you. Many people worry about:

- their spelling
- using sentences and paragraphs
- how to plan to write in the exam.

Sample questions

The questions in the exam are designed to test your skills in the areas covered by the two Assessment Objectives you have just considered.

Here are two sample questions (one for the shorter task and one for the longer task) that are typical of the exam you will take. The marks awarded for each answer are also indicated.

Shorter writing task

This is the shorter writing question:

> 1   Imagine that you are going to work in a veterinary surgery for work experience.
> <u>Write a letter</u> to the <u>senior vet</u> <u>introducing yourself</u> and <u>informing him or her about
> what job you would like to do in the surgery and why.</u>   *(16 marks)*

'Write a letter': this tells you the form the writing should take. You need to think about the language you should use. Is this a formal or informal letter? It is likely that formal (or Standard) English will be required. You need to think about how a letter is presented. This is important as some of the marks will be allocated for using the correct layout or structure for the form.

'Senior vet …': this tells you your audience (who you are writing to). You are told that your audience is a person who may be offering you work and you know their job title. You may wish to address your letter to that person by using their title or instead use the more general 'Sir or Madam', which is used for many formal letters. You should try to remember their role as you write so that the information you provide is relevant.

'Informing him or her …': this explains your main purpose in writing. The task is in three parts, keep them in mind when you plan your answer:

- introduce yourself
- inform them about a job you want
- why you think that.

A short plan will help you to focus on these details and provide a reminder of what you should include.

Activity

Look at these two examples of exam-style questions. For each one identify:

- Who is the audience for your writing?
- What is the purpose for your writing?
- Which form do you think would be most appropriate to use in your response to these questions?

> 2   Imagine you are helping to organise an end of year party at your school or college.
> Write to the manager of a local hotel explaining what type of party you want and asking for information about their facilities and prices.

> 3   You have witnessed a car accident on your way to school caused by a dog running onto the road. The dog was not hurt but the car hit a lamp-post and was damaged.
> You have been asked to write a statement about what you saw by the car owner, to send to the insurance company.

Longer writing task

The longer task will test your ability to write a non-fiction response. You will need to use your own ideas and opinions to answer this successfully. Again, you may need to be imaginative about what personal information or views you wish to include.

---

4   Explain why you **would** or **would not** enjoy having a dog. Consider:

the advantages of having a dog

the disadvantages of having one

how you feel about dogs

the effect of a dog on your lifestyle.   *(24 marks)*

What does this mean?

'Explain why' tells you that the focus of your writing should be on explaining something.

'You would or would not': This tells you that you are expected to give your opinion on the topic raised (having a dog).

You could plan your response by following the bullet points from the question. These provide a ready made structure so you should follow them to make sure that you have covered them all in your answer. Make sure that you:

- use paragraphs based on each bullet point
- varied your use of sentences
- carefully check your punctuation and spelling

Sample answers

Look again at the shorter writing task and the information about how to tackle the sample question on page 146. Now read Text A, which is a student's answer, and consider whether the student has addressed the task suitably.

> 15 Meadowview Farm
> Dalston
> Herts
>
> Dear Sir/Madam
>
> I would like to apply for a work experience placement at your vets. I am in Year 10 at Brooklands School in Dalston.
>
> I have a small amount of experience with domestic animals as I live on a farm, I have helped out with lambing and triming sheep's feet and shearing, we also have chickens that I have fed. I am going to collage one day a week and have done some work there in the small animal care unit. I have some experience in the reptile Resque department at the collage.
>
> I am particullary interested in working with a wider range of animal's as I think they would be a great challenge and exciting to work with. I feel that I am a quick learner to a challenge and am excited by the prospect of working with pet's like snake's and even horses and many more, I would be willing to help with feeding and cleaning out the animals that have been staying for an operation. I hope my enthusiasm comes across in this letter.
>
> Hope to hear from you as soon as possible with good news hopefully.
>
> Yours

Examiner's comment

The candidate has opened the letter in an appropriate way with an address and a suitable greeting. The first paragraph gives the necessary introductory information. The second paragraph does not have a range of sentence structures or punctuation and has quite limited vocabulary. It is unclear why the information about the farm and college has been included as the candidate has not made an obvious link between their experience there and the job they wish to do at the vets. The candidate has expressed their interest and enthusiasm, but this too could be expanded.

To improve the response the candidate needs to thoroughly check that their word choice is suitable for the purpose and audience. There are one or two phrases which are not entirely appropriate. They should also check the spelling and punctuation as there are several errors, for example:

- some commas are used instead of full stops
- unnecessary apostrophes on some plural words
- spelling mistakes on simple words, 'collage' and 'triming'.

The candidate should also include more detail in the section which explains which animals they wish to work with, for example, what they feel they would need to learn.

What do you think?

Read the following and make notes on your answers.

- Discuss whether you agree with the examiner's comments about the response.
- Can you identify places where the examiner may think the word choice is inappropriate?
- Have you spotted other spelling mistakes – and can you correct all of them?

Activity

2   Choose only *one* of the following:
a   Re-draft Text A. Bear in mind the comments made by the examiner about how the example could be improved.
b   Write a letter of application to a local business asking for a part-time job in an area of your choosing – for example, as a waiter/waitress in a local restaurant or as an assistant in a shop. Keep in mind the examiner's comment on Text A.

Why do I think I would enjoy having a dog? Think about these questions – Do you enjoy the comfort of an animal? Ever feel lonely and need a hug? Dogs are the answer! They are cuddly, cute, comforting and cheer you up.

Firstly, dogs are very useful as some are very talented. Hearing and seeing dogs help those who suffer from difficulties and without them people could be housebound. Miss C groves who has a hearing problem says 'Without my dog I wouldnt get out – she helps and comforts me. My dog is like my best friend.

families bond as a walk in the local park or forest could be part of a day of laughter and happiness.

Dogs are important in peoples lifes and if you dont have them, it is a lifetime opportunity you have missed!

Longer writing task

Text B is the start of the longer writing response to the sample question on page 146. Read the text and try to identify where the student has been successful in beginning to explain their views, and where you would suggest they need to focus their improvements.

Have you thought about what is successful and what you think needs improving? Now read what the examiner thought.

Examiner's comment

The candidate has opened with a direct reference to the task, but turned it into a rhetorical question. This is followed by further questions which make an invitation to the reader to think about aspects of keeping a dog which supports their viewpoint. The candidate chooses to use short direct sentences to make the impact more immediate. Using the connective 'Firstly' indicates that the candidate is intending to make a series of linked points which support their views about dogs, so they are trying to link together their writing. The third paragraph could be divided into separate points and developed more instead of putting both ideas in the same section.

Though the student has clearly tried to vary the sentences and vocabulary, there are errors which make the whole section less effective. To improve the response the candidate needs to use greater variety in their sentences. There are two occasions where a word is repeated within the same sentence – 'very' and 'just'. Punctuation needs to be improved, for example the quote should have closed speech marks at the end and apostrophes are not used at all

What do you think?

Read the following and make notes on your answers:

● Which areas did you identify that were the same ones as the examiner mentioned? Were there other things that you had not spotted?

● What advice would you give this student to help improve what has been written already?

Activity

3

Choose only one of the following tasks:

a Use the comments from the examiner to improve and expand Text B. Then, still considering the comments from the examiner, continue writing the rest of the task, which needs to address the other three bullet points listed in the sample question on page 146.

b Explain why you would or would not take part in sports on a regular basis. Think about:

● the advantages of taking part or not
● the disadvantages of taking part or not
● how you feel about sport
● the effect of sports on your life.

Check your learning

In this chapter you have:

● studied how the Assessment Objectives for writing are tested in the exam
● examined questions and answers in a sample paper
● considered how those answers could be improved
● understood ways to prepare for the exam

● recapped writing and planning skills
● understand how to identify components of exam questions
● considered how to use forms appropriate to tasks
● written responses to exam-style questions.

Making your writing skills count in the controlled assessment

Objectives

In this chapter you will:

learn more about how your writing is assessed in the controlled assessment

learn more about the tasks in the controlled assessment

read some sample answers and the teacher's comments on them.

What is controlled assessment?

During your GCSE course, the writing skills that you have developed during the first nine chapters of Section B of this book will be tested by controlled assessment. What this will involve depends on whether you are studying GCSE English or GCSE English Language.

GCSE English

Controlled assessment title:
Producing creative texts

Mark value:
40 marks = 20%

Choice of task:
Two of:

- Moving images
- Prompts and re-creations
- Me. Myself. I.

Planning and preparation:
You are allowed to spend time preparing for and planning your writing, and you may make brief notes that can be taken into the controlled assessment.

Time for writing:
Up to 4 hours.

Expected length:
About 1600 words over both pieces of writing

GCSE English Language

Controlled assessment title:
Creative writing

Mark value:
30 marks = 15%

Choice of task:
Two of:

- Moving images
- Re-creations
- Commissions

Planning and preparation:
You are allowed to spend time preparing for and planning your writing, and you may make brief notes that can be taken into the controlled assessment.

Time for writing:
Up to 4 hours

Expected length:
About 1200 words over both pieces of writing

You are allowed to take brief notes into the controlled assessment.
You are *not* allowed:

- pre-prepared drafts: you must not write out a 'rough' version of your response and either seek advice about it or take it into the controlled assessment.
- dictionaries, spell-checkers or thesauruses.
- to take your writing out of the controlled assessment room between sessions.

Introducing the tasks

There are three options for the controlled assessment task:

GCSE English

- Moving images – writing for or about moving images.
- Prompts and re-creations – using a text or prompt to developed writing.
- Me. Myself. I. – writing from personal experiences.

You will produce two pieces of writing in response to tasks from two of these categories, totalling around 1600 words across both pieces.

GCSE English Language

- Moving images – writing for or about moving images.
- Re-creations – taking a text and turning it into another.
- Commissions – responding to a given brief.

You will produce two pieces of writing in response to tasks from two of these categories, totalling around 1200 words across both pieces.

One of the most important differences between exams and controlled assessments is that you have quite a lot of time to prepare for the controlled assessment task. You will know the task – unlike in the exam – and you will be able to discuss and research it in lessons before the controlled assessment.

To do well in the controlled assessment task, you will need a good understanding of the Assessment Objectives for Writing. You will find a detailed breakdown of what each of the Assessment Objectives mean on page 145 in Chapter 22, which focuses on the writing part of the exam.

Preparing for the controlled assessment

You will be taught how to respond to the different tasks. This may include reading examples of different texts to give you ideas about structure and style. You may practise writing in different ways and have chances to discuss how your responses could be improved. You may also be given materials to take home to study and have access to resources online to help you prepare.

Whatever materials or resources you use, you will be expected to submit a record of these as part of the final controlled assessment. This will include any books, articles, TV programmes or websites.

Sample tasks and answers k!

Moving Images (GCSE English and GCSE English Language)

In this task you are invited to respond in some way to moving images such as adverts, documentaries, films, television or music videos. Here is a sample task.

> Choose one short, memorable scene from a film you have seen. Use the scene to write a creative piece in which you concentrate on creating atmosphere.

As with all creative writing tasks you have choices and decisions to make at the thinking/planning stage – for example:

- which film and scene to choose
- which form of writing to choose.

You will need to take these decisions before you move into planning the structure and style of your writing.

Activity

1

a Make a list of sections of films that remain vividly in your memory. About two or three will be plenty.

b Next to each jot down a few words to describe the atmosphere developed in the scene. To describe atmosphere you need words such as light, dark, frightening, depressing, comic, tense, dangerous, wild, happy, strange.

c Focus on the writing task: you will need to develop an atmosphere using words rather than the mixture of words, images and sounds used in films. Decide which section of film might provide the most interesting for your writing.

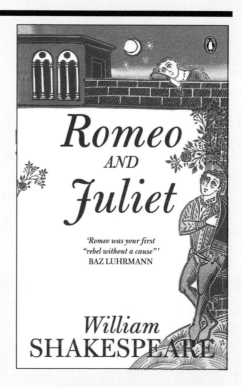

Text A is based upon the scene in Baz Luhrman's *Romeo and Juliet* when Mercutio and Benvolio are on the beach. Benvolio is worried: it is hot and there is tension in the air.

A

Ben glanced anxiously down the street. In the heat haze the air shimmered like silver water just above the tarmac; ordinary things seemed different somehow. Different.

The street was empty. Houses were shuttered up as those who lived there fought back against the all-conquering, blinding sun. Halfway down an old dog lying flat in the dust panted, ears flicking at the flies.

A beetle bustled along the base of the wall in the shade of which Ben and Merc were slouching. Ben prodded it with his toe and wondered if beetles felt heat. It barely altered course, safe in its black armour. He watched it scuttle along the base of the wall and under Merc's heel. Ben didn't hear anything as it was squashed, but he imagined a splintering squelch.

'Merc, let's go home. It's hotter than hell and you know the Caps are around.'

'Go if you want; I'm staying. You scared?'

Ben knew there was no point continuing the conversation and the heat had sapped all his energy. He glanced again down the street. A dark figure had turned the corner.

Teacher's comment

This is an engaging, effective piece of writing. The candidate keeps a good focus on the task and succeeds in creating her own individual interpretation of the scene from the film without following every detail of it. The writing is thoughtfully paragraphed with each separate paragraph focusing on a separate detail. There is a good opening short paragraph which concludes with an effective one-word sentence. There is some variety of sentence structures: the candidate uses simple sentences, for example at the start of the second paragraph; compound sentences, for example in the opening sentence of the final paragraph; and complex sentences, for example the final sentence of the second paragraph. A wide range of punctuation is used correctly.

Prompts and re-creations (GCSE English and GCSE English Language)

The task may ask you to take a text and turn it into a different form, for example, turning a script into a piece of prose. It may be based on a text you have already studied or it could be a new one given to you as part of the task. You may be told which form you should turn a text into or you may be asked to choose the form yourself.

For English, you may be asked to create some new writing based on a prompt, which could be a verse from a poem or a sentence from a novel, etc. For example, you could tell the story of a poem from a different character's point of view.

When undertaking this type of task you think carefully about what kind of writing you want to produce. Make sure you consider how to match the needs of your purpose and audience, use vocabulary for effect, vary your sentence structures for effect and organise your ideas.

Prompts and re-creations/ Re-creations

Here is a sample task based on the re-creations topic area: Read 'She Pops Home' by Cal Clothier.

> 1 Transform this text into one of your own. You might, for example, write from a different point of view or change the form.

She Pops Home

She pops home just long enough
  to overload the washing machine
  to spend a couple of hours on the phone
  to spray the bathroom mirror with lacquer
  to kick the stair-carpet out of line
  to say 'that's new—can I borrow it?'

She pops home just long enough
  to dust the aspidistra with her elbow
  to squeak her hand down the bannister
  to use the last of the toilet roll
  to leave her bite in the last apple

She pops home just long enough
  to raid her mother's drawer for tights
  to stock up with next month's pill
  to hug a tenner out of Dad

She pops home just long enough
  to horrify them with her irresponsibility
  to leave them sweating till next time

She pops home just long enough
  to light their pond like a kingfisher

She pops home just long enough

Cal Clothier, 'She Pops Home'

Having read this poem, a student chose to transform the text into an account written from the point of view of the girl referred to as 'She'. The plan included details from the poem, as well as making up some additional details such as how old the girl is, what she does, where she lives and why she does not live at home anymore. Text C is a sample answer taken from the middle of the student's response.

C

I don't mean to worry them when I pop home, but I get the feeling that after I've gone they spend the next few days fretting about me! It's not like I can't look after myself – I'm 17 after all. The thing is, it's sooo much easier to go home and use their stuff instead of going to the lorndret or using up all my phone credit. The washing piles up so quick that it would cost a fortune to get it done there. Mum doesn't mind really. I know she says she does, and last time I know she was annoyed about me taking her washing out, but she'd rather I didn't spend my hard-earned cash just on washing! It annoys her more when I nick her stuff ...

Teacher's comment

The words highlighted in pink are ideas that are in the original text. This reminds the reader that the account is adapted from a poem. By using these through the account, the structure of the writing is improved. This can be further improved by making sure that all references to things that are described in the poem are backed up by quotes from the poem.

Another feature taken from the poem (shown by the green highlights) is that about the washing. However, the student has repeated this several times in quite a short period of time, so more varied vocabulary would improve the writing. The word 'lorndret' is not spelt correctly, but phonetically it will sound the same.

Activity

2
Choose only *one* of the following options:

a Use Text C as the basis for your own writing from the viewpoint of the girl. You could write a section before the one given and another which would come after it.

b Change the form of Text B by writing a script. This could be a conversation between the girl's parents about what she is like when she 'pops' home, or between the girl and someone else. You may have other ideas about how a script could be written about the situation in the text.

Me. Myself. I. (GCSE English)

This controlled assessment task asks you to write about yourself and important experiences, people or places in your life. You will be invited to choose which form you feel is most suitable to show your ideas. Make sure that whatever form you choose will 'show-off' your skills in that area and demonstrate your ability to use vocabulary and structure to impact your reader.

The Assessment Objectives for this state that you need to 'organise information' as well as 'write clearly and imaginatively'. This means you may need to be selective with the material you use in order to meet these criteria. A considered and clear response will gain better marks than one which is longer but full of irrelevant information.

Here is a sample task based on the Me. Myself. I. topic area:

2 Write about someone who has made an impact on your life.
You can choose to write about someone you know personally or someone you think has influenced you although you have not met them. Choose a form you feel could best lead to effective writing.

This task asks you to write about someone you consider to have been important in your life. The word 'impact' suggests that you will be showing what they have done which has affected you. You should plan what to include in your answer.

The person who has had the biggest impact on my life has to be my Grandad. I chose him rather than my mum, because I think some of the things I have done with him have had a massive effect on my option choices and future career plans. He has been an inspiration to me!

Teacher's comment

The text highlighted in pink shows that the student has started with the focus on the task. The phrase 'massive effect' means much the same as 'biggest impact', but creates more interest by changing the words slightly. The student has already tried to show they are varying their vocabulary.

The section highlighted in blue is the impact that the student is going to write about. Putting that at the beginning shows the reader that the next few paragraphs will be linked to this first idea, which will show that the student is organised and has the ideas in a logical sequence.

As a third of the marks will be linked to sentence structures and punctuation, the student has chosen to show some variety in the section highlighted in green. This short sentence and exclamation mark contrasts with the longer sentence that went before it.

Activity

3 Think of a person who would be suitable to write about to answer in sample question 2. Create your own plan to show what you would include to show the impact they have had on your life. Use your plan to write the opening paragraph with some of the techniques shown.

Commissions (GCSE English Language)

In this task you will be invited to write for a specific audience and purpose. The tasks may be linked with writing for particular media. You will be given the chance to express your own ideas in a particular form. For example, you may be asked to write an article, or to create a web page, on a topic of interest. You may be set a word limit. Think carefully about matching the needs of your purpose and audience, using vocabulary for effect, varying your sentence structures for effect and organising your ideas.

Here is a sample task based on the Commissions topic area:

3 You have been contacted by the owner of a web site that provides a platform for people to explain their interests to a wider audience. One section of the site is called 'Passions'. Some writers use the section to explain their strongly-held views, while others explain something they enjoy doing. You have been asked to write no more than 750 words about your own passion. Write your piece for this web page.

The student who chose to do this task decided to write about cricket. Text F below is his first draft.

Read it through and think about what he needs to do with this text to improve it. Think about the assessment objectives this writing is addressing.

Does it show:

- organised sentences and paragraphs with correct spelling and punctuation
- clear and imaginative writing with carefully chosen vocabulary
- paragraphs that are coherent and varied sentence structures?

What advice would you give the student to help him improve his writing?

My passion is sport and cricket is one of my favourite sports, I first got involved in cricket because my dad played cricket for his local team. The reason I enjoy cricket is that everybody in the team has an individual job to do, to make the team successful in the match. I also like it because if you fail at batting, you can do well at bowling so there are plenty of opportunities for everyone to have a go and do well.

There is different forms of cricket some are limited overs there is 20 overs which is a quick scoring game, then there is 40 and 50 overs that is quick scoring when the powerplay is introduced but it is not so quick without powerplay. Then there is test match cricket which is very very slow but see's players get big scores. My favourite to watch is 40 overs and is also my favourite to play.

Activity

4   Choose only *one* of the following options:

a   Pick a topic that you feel strongly about to write your own web page entitled: 'Passion'. If you are able to use ICT for this, you may want to consider how you wish to present your ideas as if on a web page.

b   You have been asked to write for a magazine aimed at teenagers. The title of the piece is 'Pet Hates'. You can make this serious or amusing, but it should appeal to young people through its form and content.

Check your learning

In this chapter you have:

- learnt about how your writing skills are tested in the controlled assessment
- looked at sample tasks and answers and how they can be improved.

Speaking and listening

Getting started

Discuss the following with a partner:

- Do you consider yourself to be good at speaking in class, in groups, in front of strangers?
- Are you good at presenting, making a speech or giving a talk?
- Do you enjoy drama-based activities?
- Are you a good listener?
- Explain what you like and/or dislike about speaking and listening.
- Why do you think speaking and listening are considered to be such important skills?

Aims of the Speaking and listening section

The qualification you are studying will equip you to use your speaking and listening skills in a range of situations, including:

- school and college courses after GCSEs
- work-based learning
- business communications such as meetings and interviews
- personal communications.

There will be opportunities for you to use the skills you already have, but also to extend and develop these in new directions. Working with other students, you will be encouraged to try out new ideas and help them to improve their skills too.

Does this all sound a bit 'too much'?

Don't worry. You will not be expected to do all of this straightaway. The tasks are intended to help you gradually improve your ability to tackle different forms of speaking and listening, and work on each aspect so you have the chance to build up your confidence.

Activities

In this section of the book, you will learn what makes a good speaker and a good listener, and how to use your skills in pairs, small groups, in presenting to others and in drama-based work. This work will enable you to adapt the way you speak and listen according to the task and the people you are talking to. You will also become a better, more active listener and more able to perform well in the different tasks for assessment that you will have to do.

Assessments

The chapters each address differing aspects of the GCSE course. At the start of each chapter, you will know what area you are going to be working on.

There is one form of assessment for speaking and listening:

- controlled assessment.

You will be given tasks that have to be done in class. These will be set by your teacher and will be worth up to 20 per cent of the final mark.

24 Your speaking and listening skills

Objectives

In this chapter you will:

learn about good speaking skills

learn about good listening skills

learn about the use of body language.

In this chapter you will think about the skills needed to be a good speaker and listener in different situations. You will also think about your own skills as a speaker and listener and work out what you need to do to improve.

You will be looking at the following issues:

- What makes a good speaker?
- What makes a good listener?
- Facial expression and body language.

Activity

1.
a. With a partner, look at the cartoons below and talk about the facial expression and body language.
b. Now think about your reasons. Which details show good skills and which show bad skills? Make a list of your reasons.

What makes a good speaker?

When we speak, we communicate our ideas to others by the words we use and our tone of voice. Equally important are our facial expressions and body language. Remember, the focus here is on *how* you present your ideas as much as *what* you are saying.

Activities

2
a Read through the points below. They are all features of being a good speaker.

A good speaker:
- plans what they are going to say
- respects the views of others
- explains their ideas fully
- chooses their words to match the audience and purpose
- varies their volume, pace and expression.

b With a partner, add any more qualities of a good speaker you can think of to this list.

c Decide which you think are the most important qualities, note them down on a 'Top five tips for good speakers' list.

3 Now it is time to practise what you have learned about good speakers.

a Think about an activity or a day out that you enjoyed in the last two weeks. Use your 'Top five tips for good speakers' to prepare a one-minute talk about it that you will give to your partner in class. One minute is not a long time so, before you start, you might want to make some notes about the key things that you want to tell your partner.

b Present your talk to your partner.

c Listen to your partner's talk.

d Discuss with your partner how well you each used the 'Top five tips for good speakers' and offer advice for improvement.

> ### Review and reflect
> Based on the feedback your partner gave you in Activity 3d, make a note of:
> - one thing that you have done well
> - one target for improvement in the next speaking task that you do.

What makes a good listener?

One of the most important things in sharing and developing ideas and opinions is how well you listen to other people. Active listening means that, when someone else is talking, you need to:
- pay attention to what is being said
- encourage, support and agree with what others are saying
- challenge and question what others are saying in a *positive* way.

Activities

4 The following points are some of the characteristics a good listener might have:

- maintains eye contact with the speaker
- listens carefully
- tries not to interrupt
- respects the views of others
- thinks about what others say.

a With a partner, add any more characteristics you can think of to this list.

b Now agree your 'Top five tips for good listeners'.

5 **a** Work in pairs. You are both going to prepare and present a short talk. You will then listen to each other's talk. Follow these steps:

- Use your 'Top five tips for good speakers' to prepare a one-minute talk about your favourite TV show or a film you saw recently. Make sure you have five interesting details – for example, the names of the main characters.
- Take it in turn to listen carefully to each other's talk. Think of three questions to ask your partner about their chosen TV show or film.
- Ask your questions and listen carefully to the answers.
- Give yourself a grade from A to E depending on how well you think you listened.

b As you listen to your partner's talk, use your 'Top 5 tips for good listeners'. Discuss the talk your partner gave and the five facts that you noted down. Ask your partner the three questions you have about their talk.

c Repeat the activity so that your partner has an opportunity to speak, listen and give feedback.

Body language

The term 'body language' is used to describe the non-verbal ways we communicate with others. For example, we might:

- nod or shake our heads to show we agree or disagree
- smile
- make eye contact
- lean forward to show we are paying close attention to what is being said
- use **gestures** to emphasise a point.

We often use gestures to make what we are saying clearer. It sometimes helps to work out what people really think by watching their body language.

Key terms

Gesture: a movement of the hands, head or body to express or emphasise an idea or emotion.

Activities

6 Look at cartoons A, B and C and make a note of what you think the body language suggests in each one. Share your ideas with a partner and update your notes if you need to.

7 Now you are going to practise using body language. Think of something that you have enjoyed doing at school in the past week or two. Talk to your partner about what you enjoyed and why. Aim to match what you are saying with the appropriate body language.

Evaluating your skills

Activity

8 Have you got what it takes to be a good speaker and listener? Complete this quick questionnaire to find out:

❶ **You have been asked to give a presentation to the class. Do you feel:**
   (a) Terrified? You often find it difficult to organise your ideas and to speak in detail in front of a large group.
   (b) Confident? You enjoy the challenge of communicating your ideas and issues in detail and promoting your point of view to a large group.
   (c) Slightly nervous at first? However, you are quite confident you can communicate your ideas clearly.

❷ **After listening to a presentation in class do you usually:**
   (a) Have lots of questions to ask because you find it interesting to listen to the ideas of other students and want to find out more?
   (b) Find it quite easy to follow the main ideas and ask questions?
   (c) Find it hard to concentrate and let other people ask the questions because you can never think of anything to ask?

❸ **When you take part in a group discussion do you:**
   (a) Enjoy responding to the ideas of others and making suggestions that move the discussion forward?
   (b) Make one or two points, but feel more comfortable agreeing with points made by others?
   (c) Enjoy challenging the ideas of others and introducing new points to the discussion?

❹ **If you are asked to assume the role of a character in a role play do you:**
   (a) Present the kind of character that is very predictable – for example, a bad-tempered teacher?
   (b) Enjoy creating an individual character by using appropriate body language?
   (c) Give some thought to how you will use language and body language to create your character?

❺ **When you are taking part in a speaking and listening task do you:**
   (a) Consider the audience and purpose and choose a wide range of vocabulary and sentence structures to match these?
   (b) Use vocabulary and sentence structures to match audience and purpose?
   (c) Try to use some variety of vocabulary but often fall back on the vocabulary you normally use?

Activity

How did you do? Use the table below to score points for each question. Add up your points before checking your total against the speaking and listening profiles below.

Questions	(a)	(b)	(c)
1	1	3	2
2	3	2	1
3	2	1	3
4	1	3	2
5	3	2	1

14–15
You are well on the way to becoming a very effective speaker and listener. You have a wide range of vocabulary that you can adapt to the needs of your audience and purpose. You are a very good listener who can develop and sustain a discussion. You adapt very well to the different roles, using words and body language to create convincing characters who have an impact on the audience.

11–13
You are a confident speaker and listener. You are successful in adapting your vocabulary to suit your audience and purpose. You change your tone of voice and vary your pace to add interest to your speech. You make significant contributions to discussions. In role play you use body language and speech to create convincing characters.

8–10
You are a reasonably confident speaker and listener. You choose your words carefully when communicating with your audience and can interest your audience by thinking about your vocabulary. You are a careful listener who takes an active part in group discussions, sometimes challenging the ideas of others. In role-play activities you use language and body language to create characters.

5–7
You have some confidence as a speaker and listener. However, you sometimes might find it hard to adapt your vocabulary to your audience and purposes. You are more comfortable as a listener than a speaker in group discussions. You are able to create a simple role successfully.

How can I improve my speaking and listening skills?

Read the following letters from students explaining some of the problems they have with improving their speaking and listening skills.

D

Dear Andy,

I really enjoy English lessons, especially the ones where we take part in group discussions. However, my friends (and also my teacher) tell me I talk too much and I don't let other people have their say. I think they may be right, but I enjoy putting forward my ideas so much that sometimes it's hard to stop.

What do you think I should do?

A chatty Year 10 student.

E

Dear Andy,

I am a very shy student. Although I always get good marks for written English tasks, I don't do very well at the Speaking and listening ones. The ones I really can't do are the individual presentations to my class. It doesn't matter if I am with a group saying something on my own or, worse, standing in front of the class doing a solo presentation, I always do badly.

There are quite a few things that I just can't do. I find it hard to keep eye contact with the audience as I feel safer if I read my bit as fast as possible so I can sit down again. I find it hard to prepare the presentation in the first place, as the fact that I'm going to have to talk in front of the class is really scary so I can never think of good ideas. Also, I'm not good with choosing the right words for my audience when it comes to speaking tasks.

I would really like to do something about this so that I can do better in my speaking and listening tasks. What can you suggest?

A shy Year 11 student

F

Dear Andy,

I wonder if you can help me? The thing I hate most about speaking and listening tasks is doing the role play. I'm not good at drama and these sorts of tasks are horrible, I'm just no good at performing. I usually let the rest of the group decide the role I will play and then I end up standing on the spot and saying my bit as quickly as possible. Most of the time I end up being the character who is cross and shouts a lot like a policeman or a bad-tempered parent. In the role play interviews, I can never think of good questions to ask or answers to give.

I hope you can offer some ideas to help me, as the rest of my group are much better than me and I would like to be as good as they are.

A self-conscious Year 11 student

Activity

9 Here is the reply to letter D:

Dear chatty Year 10 student,

I'm sure your friends love you really! However, you have to remember that you are not only assessed at GCSE for your speaking skills, but also for your listening skills. Don't worry; it is possible to train yourself to be a good listener.

Perhaps in group discussions you could ask your teacher if you could take the role of chairperson. This would mean that your role would be to encourage other students to speak and this would give you good practice in listening to their ideas.

You could also ask someone in the group to be your 'critical friend' – someone who points out what you are doing well and how you need to improve. They could make a note of the number of times you carry on speaking when other students are trying to give their point of view. Next time there is a group discussion you could try to cut down this number.

Maybe you need to work on the language you use in discussions. For example, after you have made your point, you could invite other students to comment on your ideas saying something like, 'What do the rest of you think?'

I hope you do well at listening in the future.

Take care,

Andy

a With a partner, discuss letters E and F and suggest ideas on what each writer could try to do to improve.

b Share your suggestions with another pair and see whether you have suggested the same things. You may want to update your suggestions after this.

Check your learning

In this chapter you have:

- learned about the skills that make a good speaker
- learned about the skills that make a good listener
- practised your listening skills
- identified your strengths as a speaker and listener
- thought about how you can improve your speaking and listening
- made suggestions to others on how they can improve their skills.

25 Presentation

Objectives

In this chapter you will:

the key features which help to make a 'good' presentation

how to plan, prepare and deliver a presentation.

One of your assessments at GCSE will be based on a presentation you give. Being able to present is a key **functional skill** and it may involve one of the following:

- explaining a process to others
- giving a clear account of something that has happened
- persuading or advising others.

Key terms

Functional skill: A skill which enables people to operate effectively in the work place and in social situations.

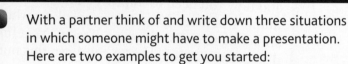

Activity

1
With a partner think of and write down three situations in which someone might have to make a presentation. Here are two examples to get you started:

- in a school assembly
- demonstrating a new piece of equipment.

What makes a good presentation?

You need to understand the key features that make a good presentation so that you can use them when you prepare your own presentations. These key features fall into four broad headings:

- Organisation
- Vocabulary
- Standard English
- Response.

Activity

2

You are going to prepare and give a presentation informing your audience about a topic you are interested in. Your audience is students of your own age and their teachers. Your presentation should last for 3–5 minutes. The following sections take you through the preparation you need to make before giving your presentation. Keep the notes you make in each activity to help you with your final presentation.

Organisation

A good presentation will be well organised. To organise your presentation you need to think about:

- **Content:** The key points you want to cover. Do not try to cover too much! You should include information that is relevant to your particular audience. For example, in a talk about a hobby you could explain why teenagers might find it an interesting pastime.
- **Order:** The order in which you present your key points. What key point does your audience need first to understand the rest of the presentation? What do they need to know after that?
- **Timing:** the time available for your presentation. In this case you have 3–5 minutes. It is important that all key points are clearly made without rushing.

You might find you want to consider using one of the following methods to organise your presentation:

- PowerPoint or other presentation software: use this to highlight a key point or enhance what you say with an image or an audio clip.
- Visual stimuli such as photographs, illustrations or maps.
- Note cards or prompt cards: make notes of your key points that will act as prompts. Keep these short and simple so that you can follow them easily when you are talking!

Activity

3

a Decide on the topic for your presentation. Make sure you choose something you know about and can talk about in an interesting way. It could be something as ordinary as 'My Family' or as unusual as 'The Life of Moles'.

b Decide the key points you will make. List them. Remember that your aim is to inform your audience.

c Now decide on the order in which you will speak about your key points. Aim to grab your audience's attention right from the start. Number your key points in your chosen order.

d Decide how long you will spend talking about each key point. Write the approximate time in seconds or minutes next to each one. Make sure that the total is between 3 and 5 minutes.

Vocabulary

The range and appropriateness of the words used in a presentation is an important feature of its success. You need to think about:

- Audience: your presentation needs to be aimed at students your age so the words you choose need to be suitable for them.

- Purpose: your aim is to inform your audience so the words you choose need to help you to do this. Good use of descriptive words can help your audience to visualise what you are talking about.

- Technical/specialist language: you may need to use technical terms but you may also need to explain these to your audience.

Activity k!

4

a Remind yourself of your chosen topic and your key points (Activity 3). For each key point list three descriptive words that would help your reader to visualise what you are talking about.

b List any technical or specialist words that you might use and beside each one make a note of how you would explain this word.

c Make a note of:
- the words you will use to start your presentation
- the words you will use to link each key point to the one that has come before it
- the words you will use to end your presentation.

d Listed below is a range of words that you might find helpful to include in your presentation. Copy the ones that you think might be useful to you and make a note of where you might use them.

fascinating	amazing	difficult	challenging	popular
unique	brilliant	exhausting	demanding	
satisfying	rewarding	embarrassing	stimulating	
mystifying	spectacular	routine	entertaining	
revolutionary	distressing			

Using a range of language

The purpose of presentations is to deliver information and opinions to your audience in ways that engage them.

You will need to use a range of vocabulary and language structures in different situations for different purposes. High levels of performance will require a range of 'well-judged' and 'flexible' vocabulary and expression.

Read Texts A and B, annotated versions of two alternative openings to a presentation in which a student was asked to talk about favourite films to the rest of the class.

MATT DAMON
THE
BOURNE ULTIMATUM
THIS SUMMER BOURNE COMES HOME

A

Morning. I'm going to talk about the Bourne films. There are three Bourne films. The first is *The Bourne Identity*. The second is *The Bourne Supremacy* and the last is *The Bourne Ultimatum*. The films are about Jason Bourne who is played by Matt Damon in the three films. *The Bourne Identity* came out in 2002. *The Bourne Supremacy* came out in 2004 and *The Bourne Ultimatum* came out in 2007.

An appropriate concise beginning

Another sentence which begins, boringly, with 'The ...'. The student, for the sake of a little variety, could have said: 'Matt Damon stars as the hero, Jason Bourne, in all three'

This is clear but it is another very short sentence. The student could simply have said 'I'm going to talk about the three Bourne films'

This becomes a very boring list. The student could have said, 'In order they are ...' or, if the list was to be kept, instead of 'The second is' some variety could have been added by simply saying, 'followed by ...'

Another repetition of the film titles in another very dull list. It would have been better to put the date information in the earlier list to avoid this kind of dull repetition

B

Good morning. I'm going to talk about the greatest, most spectacular, downright brilliant series of films in the history of movies. It must be *Lord of the Rings*, you're thinking. Wrong. Well, it must be *Harry Potter*. Ouch, no! Well, that leaves James Bond. Sorry, they're not fit to lick the boots of ... Jason Bourne in the three superb Bourne films.

A one-word sentence used for effect. The student uses a sequence of possible films followed by concise put-downs

Not Standard English, but the slang is perfectly appropriate for the audience and the kind of jokey tone the student is adopting

The student doesn't go for the obvious kind of opening but delays the information. Three adjectives are listed to jokingly build up expectations

The student uses second person to acknowledge the listeners

A simple point, but the student has found a different word from 'great', 'spectacular', 'brilliant'

5

a Building on the vocabulary you chose in the previous activity write the introduction to your presentation – no more than four or five lines. You could also try out some of the techniques used in Text B: not giving away the topic of your speech straight away, addressing your audience directly, and using one word sentences for effect.

b Try your introduction out on a partner and get them to give you feedback on:

- How well you used a range of language.
- How interesting they found your introduction.

Standard English

Standard English is used in most presentations. Remind yourself of the following details about Standard English:

- Standard English refers to the forms of words and grammar which would be recognised and understood in any part of the UK.
- If someone speaks in Standard English, you cannot tell where they come from based on their vocabulary and grammar – although their accent might give you a clue.
- Standard English is the form of English which tends to be used in formal situations at work. You are assessed on your ability to use Standard English in your controlled assessments for GCSE.

A presentation requires a greater use of Standard English than, for example, a discussion because it is more formal. The context, purpose and audience of a presentation will give you an idea of how much Standard English should be used. For example, a presentation to the Chair of Governors is likely to require Standard English usage throughout. In a presentation to other students, however, you might want to mix Standard and non-Standard English.

6

Think about each of the following presentation scenarios. Decide whether Standard English should be used throughout or whether a mix of Standard and non-Standard English might be more appropriate. For each one, give the reasons for your decision

a A presentation to parents by the Head Teacher informing them about the school's recent progress.

b A presentation of a new product to local people in a shopping centre.

c A presentation in assembly by Year 11 students to Year 9 students encouraging them to support a particular charity.

d A presentation by Year 11 students to parents explaining why they should send their children to that school.

e A presentation by an applicant for a job in business demonstrating why s/he should be appointed.

f A presentation by a politician to be broadcast live on TV.

g A presentation by a student informing other students on a topic that interests him or her.

Well it's like this innit.

Response

Many presentations end with an invitation to the audience to ask questions. To get the best marks for your presentation you need to:

- Show you understand why the question is being asked.
- Answer it using relevant details from your talk or your knowledge.

You might find it helps to think in advance about the questions that you might be asked and how you could answer them.

Below is a copy of the notes one student made for a presentation on a topic he was interested in: fitness. The final row shows the questions he anticipated being asked and his prepared answers.

Key feature	Planning notes
Organisation	1. statistics about unfit teenagers – 30 seconds 2. fitness-a balance of healthy eating and exercise – 30 seconds 3. how calories work – intake – values in different foods – differences for men and women – 1 minute 4. exercise – amount needed – suggestions for activities – costs (time/money) – 1 minute 5. benefits of a healthy lifestyle – 1 minute 6. my personal fitness plan – 1 minute
Vocabulary	• Needs to be appropriate to teenagers • Needs to inform and interest • Start with: Do you realise that … Links: It's not just a matter of … It doesn't take much to … You too can make a difference … • Might need to explain: calories / calorific values; cardio-vascular; aerobic • fibre – fat – saturated fat – poly-unsaturated fat; vitamins.
Standard English	• Presentation for teenagers and teenagers – mainly Standard English – may use occasional non-standard words
Response to possible questions	• Why shouldn't I just diet? Exercise can improve all round health and fitness levels. • Is it best to join a group or club? Depends on the individual but some people find it more motivating to exercise with others. Others prefer to work alone. • Why does fitness matter if I am slim and look ok? Refer to health benefits.

Activity

7 Remind yourself of your chosen topic and your key points (Activity 3). Write down three questions that you could be asked. Beside each question write the answer you would give.

Making your presentation

So far in this chapter, you have made notes on content, vocabulary, use of Standard English and the questions you might be answered and the answers you would give to them. You are almost ready to make your presentation. First allow yourself time to rehearse your presentation. Try to run through it several times so that you feel comfortable saying it and familiar with the content. Here are some other important tips that will help you to do well:

- look at your audience when you speak
- speak clearly and make sure you can be heard by all your audience
- pace yourself, do not speak too quickly
- vary your tone of voice
- do not read your presentation from notes
- consider using visual stimuli such as PowerPoint or photographs, maps and equipment.

Activity

8 Now you need to make your presentation.

Ask two or three students in the audience to use the criteria below to give you feedback on your performance. Use their feedback to help you set targets for improvement for your next presentation.

- presentation is clearly organised and focused
- vocabulary used is varied and appropriate to the audience
- Standard English is used confidently and where appropriate
- questions are answered using relevant and effective detail.

Check your learning

You have been asked to make a presentation to pupils at a local primary school to tell them why they should choose to come to your secondary school.

With a partner, discuss and make notes on the presentation you would give using the following headings to help you:

- Organisation
- Vocabulary
- Standard English
- Questions and responses

26

Discussing and listening

Throughout the course, you will have many opportunities to take part in group activities. These activities will allow you to share your thoughts and opinions on a range of issues to inform and shape the ideas of other members of the group, as well as make your own thinking clearer.

Being a good group member

Successful group work is based on:

- the contributions made by group members to the development of the discussion
- the ways in which group members are listened to
- the ways in which group members interact with each other.

There are many ways in which you can contribute to group work. These include:

1 Making suggestions.
2 Expressing a point of view.
3 Asking questions.
4 Drawing some of the ideas together.
5 Supporting the view of others.
6 Challenging the views of others.

Printed on page 174 are some extracts taken from classroom talk. In each case, the class was working in groups.

1 With a partner, find examples from the extracts below that match the six points listed. You might find that some of the extracts match more than one of the six points on page 173. Keep a record of your ideas.

a Let's look at the … first.

b Should we try to sort out the … now?

c I think we should …

d My view is that …

e The best way to do that is to …

f Does anyone else think that …?

g What do you think … means?

h We all seem to be saying that …

i Both of those poems are saying that …

j That's right. I also think that …

k Yes. There is another example as well. Remember …

l I'm not sure I agree. What about …?

m Surely not. If that were true, then how would …?

> **Top tip**
>
> As you take part in the other group tasks during your course, practise using some of the phrases in the speech bubbles in Activity 1 to help you contribute to discussions.

Asking the right questions

Some people find it easy to ask lots of questions when they are listening to someone speak. Knowing how to ask the right sort of question is a very useful skill to have. There are two different kinds of question you can ask:

Closed questions are questions that can usually be answered with just a few words. For example, the question 'Did you have a good weekend?' can be answered with a simple 'Yes' or a 'No'.

Open questions are questions that invite the speaker to explain something more clearly or tell you more about it. For example, the question 'What did you do at the weekend?' encourages a detailed and developed answer.

At times you might also want to combine a closed and an open question – for example, 'Did you have a good weekend? What did you do?'

Activities

2 You have been listening to a friend tell you about a film they saw at the weekend. List two closed and two open questions you could ask to help you find out more about the film. Here are two examples to help you:

> Who played the main part? (closed)

> That sounds good – what was the story about? (open)

3 In pairs, take it in turns to each talk for up to 30 seconds about what you did last weekend. Once your partner has finished talking, ask them questions to find out more. Focus on asking open questions as your aim is to help your partner give more detailed information.

When you have each had a chance to ask questions, talk about:

- whether all the questions you asked were open
- how useful the questions were in helping the speaker to give more details
- whether you found it easy or difficult to ask open questions.

Working with others

Sometimes working in groups can be difficult. We do not always agree. Sometimes we feel that others are completely wrong about something we are discussing. We need to remember, however, that each person has a right to his or her opinion.

Whether you agree or disagree with what is being said, you should aim to:
- be polite – each member of the group has a right to say what they think
- listen to others' opinions without interrupting
- encourage everyone in the group to give their opinion.

When you are working in groups you will also need to make sure you:
- keep on topic and to time limits
- discuss all relevant points
- summarise different points that are made
- draw the discussion to a conclusion.

In order to make sure these things happen, groups sometimes nominate one person as the chairperson who will be responsible for these tasks.

4

a Join up with another pair or work in small groups. You have ten minutes in which to discuss and complete one of the following tasks:

- Discuss and then choose and list in priority order five things that could be done to improve your school.

- Discuss and then choose and list in order of priority five things that are needed to form a good friendship.

- Once your group has chosen its task, spend a few minutes individually jotting down the points you want to make and think about how you can make them most effectively.

b Choose one member of your group to act as chairperson and to begin the discussion. As well as co-ordinating the work of the group, that person should make sure the task is complete within the ten minutes.

c Look back at the bullet points above. Assess how well you have done individually and as a group.

Putting it together

You are now going to use what you have learned to help you discuss a wider issue. Read the following:

The Coleridge Centre used to be a busy thriving shopping centre. However, many shoppers are staying away and some of the shops are beginning to struggle. When asked why they no longer visit the centre, many of the older shoppers said it was because of the young people who go there. Here are some of the things they said:

> Sometimes, when I see a group of youngsters standing around it makes me feel very nervous about walking past them.

> I think they shouldn't be allowed into the centre unless they are with an adult.

> I don't like it when they gather at the doorway of my shop because it puts people off coming inside. It affects my business.

> The place is so dirty. Litter is everywhere and the toilets are disgusting.

> They look so awful with their hoods over their heads and playing loud music.

> When groups of lads go around together, they can be quite loud and seem a bit threatening.

> I don't blame the youngsters. There's nowhere else to go.

> There's shops, boarded up and empty. It's depressing.

> I used to take my grandchildren there. They loved the soft-play area. But that's all gone now.

Activity

5

You are part of a group responsible for the successful running of the Coleridge Centre and you need to suggest some measures you might take to ensure shoppers of all ages continue to go there. In groups, you are going to:

- Discuss the concerns expressed by some older shoppers. What alternative points of view might be expressed by the young people who go there?

- Make suggestions for ideas to ensure the centre is a place where everyone can go. You will need to agree on these in order to come up with an action plan.

Before you begin your discussion:

- Spend some time individually planning what you want to say – you might find it helpful to use a planning table like the one above to organise your thoughts.

- Remind yourself of how to ask open and closed questions and how to work effectively with others.

- Choose one person to act as chairperson. The chairperson should remind themselves of their tasks using the guidance on page 175.

You have fifteen minutes to discuss the issues and come up with an action plan.

Review and reflect

At the end of your discussion assess your contribution to the group discussion by answering the following questions:

- Did I take an active part in the discussion?
- Did I speak clearly?
- Did I stay on task?
- Was I polite, even when I disagreed?
- Was I assertive rather than aggressive?
- Did I listen to others and ask useful questions?
- Did I support other people's ideas?

For each question give yourself a score based on your performance in the discussion:

- 1 = I think I did well.
- 2 = I did well, but I need to do some more work on this.
- 3 = I tried hard, but I need to do a lot more work on this.

Check your learning

1 What different things are needed for a group discussion to be successful?

2 What are:
- Your personal strengths in group discussion?
- Your two personal targets for improvement in group discussion?

27

Role play

What is role play?

This aspect of your assessment for Speaking and listening requires you to perform in a role, either as part of a group or individually. For your assessment, the term 'role' will always be connected to 'character'. You will be expected to create that character and then use different techniques to maintain and develop him or her.

To be convincing as the character you will need to have a good understanding of the following:

Key terms

Motivation: The reasons people have for speaking and behaving in the ways they do.

- Background: gender, age, social situation.
- Personality: thoughts, feelings, manner of speaking, body language.
- **Motivation:** ways of responding to other people and reacting in different situations and the reasons for these.

Activity

1   Work in pairs.

a   Which of these facial expressions or gestures might be used to show the following feelings?

> **Feelings**: surprise; anger; sadness; pleasure
>
> **Expressions/gestures**: clenched teeth and fists; smile; wide eyes /raised eyebrows; frown

b   What other facial expressions or gestures do you use to show your feelings?

c   Think about the feelings surprise, anger, sadness, pleasure. How would you vary the tone of your voice to show these different feelings when saying each of the following words?

Words: What   No   Really   Goodbye

d   What sort of facial expressions and gestures might you use for the following characters?

- a sulky teenager
- someone who's just been told they've won the lottery
- someone receiving very bad news
- someone telling a lie
- someone who has been accused of something but is claiming to be innocent.

e   In turns, role play one of the characters listed in **d** above. Aim to stay 'in character' for 30 seconds.

Planning a role play

Although this role play will be **improvised** (that is, not **scripted**), you will still need to prepare for it. You will need to think carefully about:

- the character you are creating
- the situation the character finds themselves in
- how your character will react to that situation.

Creating a character

One way to create a character is through a character plan. Read the following **scenario**.

Key terms

Improvised: where everything that is to happen or be spoken is *not* written down in advance.

Scripted: where everything that is to happen or be spoken is written down in advance.

Scenario: an outline of a situation, setting and the characters involved.

```
Setting: the manager's office in a
large department store.

Situation: a police officer has
just arrived to speak with the
manager and a suspected shoplifter
about an incident that took place
an hour earlier.
```

Characters:

- Shoplifter – a mother or father aged 27 accused of stealing some children's clothing.
- The store manager – a middle-aged person.
- The police officer.

Character plan

Character	Background	Personality	Motivation	Feelings and attitudes
Shoplifter	• Unemployed • Short of money • Single parent	• A caring mother/father • Proud – finds it hard to ask for help • Normally law-abiding	• Desperate • Child about to start primary school • Wants the best for the child	• Feeling isolated • Frightened • Ashamed • Worried about what other people might think
Store manager				
Police officer				

The information given in the character plan shows how the character of the shoplifter has been developed. This would help the student to role play the character and improvise the scene.

In this sort of performance, there are no right or wrong ways to develop the character. Different groups might see the characters in different ways, for example, another group could plan the shoplifter's character as a hardened, serial offender with a bad attitude. This would then have a direct impact on the way the improvisation developed.

2 Work in groups of three.

a Decide on whether you want to change or keep the character of the shoplifter as it appears in the table on the previous page. Make a copy of the table with any changes you want to make.

b Now think about the characters of the store manager and the police officer. Jot down ideas about what they could be like and how they might react in this situation. Here are a few suggestions for feelings and attitudes to get you started: angry/sympathetic/irritated/bored/helpful/concerned.

c Once you have a clear picture in your minds about these two characters, complete a character plan in your table.

Planning the scene

Once you have considered your character, you need to think about:

- **Audience**: who will be watching your role play? For example, is it your teacher, a small group of students, the whole class or someone from outside the school?

- **Purpose**: what message do you want to convey? How do you want your audience to react to the situation? For example, do you want them to be sympathetic towards the shoplifter or do you want them to see him/her as someone who deserves to be dealt with very harshly?

- **Structure**: how you will begin your role play and any key points you want to cover during it.

Here is an example of how one group decided to plan the scenario given to you earlier:

> We wanted to present a scene that seemed very like real life, but at the same time we wanted to get across to the audience, very clearly, the store's policy of: 'We always prosecute shoplifters. No exceptions.'
>
> Our starting point was the arrival of the police officer who was going to ask what had happened. The store manager and shoplifter both had a chance to make their cases, but it ended with the suspect being taken off to the police station. We knew that some people in our audience would not be sympathetic to a person in this situation. Our aim was to get them to understand that sometimes people are driven to do the wrong thing for good reasons, so we decided to stress the caring aspect of the shoplifter's character and the fact that he was unemployed. We wanted them to see that situations like this are not really 'black and white'. We spent a few minutes discussing the possibilities for how the situation might develop before we began.

Activity

3 Work in groups of three.

You are going to create a role play based on the senario described earlier. Before you do, talk about and jot down ideas on the following:

- **Audience**: who are they and how aware are they of situations like this and the issues involved?
- **Purpose**: what are the key points you want to make?
- **Structure**: how will you begin your role play and make sure you get your key points across?

You are now ready to perform your role play.

Review and reflect

Once you have carried out your role play, think about the following:

- Did I stay in role throughout the performance?
- Did I use appropriate gestures?
- Did I change my tone of voice to show thoughts and feelings?
- Did I interact with other people in the group?
- As a group, did we get our key points across?
- How did the audience react?

For each point above, give yourself a score based on your own performance in the role play:

- 1 = I think I did well at this.
- 2 = I did well, but I need to do some more work on this.
- 3 = I tried hard, but I need to do a lot more work on this.

Preparing your own role play

Now you are going to use what you have learnt in this chapter to create a role play of your own based on one of the following scenarios:

- Two friends talking about the fact that one of them has just broken up with his/her boyfriend/girlfriend.
- Two parents discussing their concerns about their child's behaviour.
- A parent and child talking about the child being allowed to go to stay at a friend's house for the weekend.
- A teacher and student discussing a bullying incident.

Activity

4
a With a partner, choose which of the scenarios you want to perform.
b Use the character plan table on page 179 to develop the characters in your role play.
c Make sure you know the audience for your role play.
d Decide on the structure of your role play. How are you going to start? What key points do you want to make?

Practice makes perfect!

One way to improve your role play is to practise. This means you need to:

- rehearse the sorts of things your character is going to say
- understand the role you are playing
- understand the situation your character is in.

Rehearsal allows you to try out the order and timing of events and speeches. Before you start to practise your role play, think about:

- speaking clearly, so that your audience will be able to follow what you are saying
- varying your tone of voice to show your thoughts and feelings
- how you will use body language, including facial expressions to show your thoughts and feelings
- the importance of staying in role throughout the performance to help make the character(s) believable.

Activity

a Using the bullet points above to help you, rehearse your role play so that you can practise developing your character.

b You are now going to present your role play to another pair. At the end of the role play, you will use the following criteria to assess how you did:

- Was your character well developed?
- Was your role play convincing?
- Was your delivery clear and well paced?
- Did you use tone of voice effectively?
- Did you use body language effectively?
- Did your role play begin and end effectively?

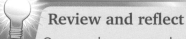

Review and reflect

Once you have assessed yourself, make a note of two things you did well and two things you will aim to improve in your next role play.

For each point above, give yourself a score based on your own performance (as you did for the Review and reflect on page 181):

1 I think I did well at this.

2 I did well, but I need to do some more work on this.

3 I tried hard, but I need to do a lot more work on this.

A final thought

You might be asked to create a role play based on a text you have studied. This means that you will be expected to play a character that has already been developed by the writer. In these circumstances, you will not need to create the character yourself but you will need to make sure you clearly understand the character the writer has created. You still need to:

- understand the character's motivation
- consider how the character reacts in the situation in which he/she has been placed by the writer and/or the additional context decided by your teacher.

Techniques you could use to show your understanding of a character include:

- **Hot seating:** this is where you take the role of a character and answer questions from the audience about:
  - his or her life
  - the things that have happened to him or her, or may happen in the future
  - thoughts and feelings about his or her experiences.
- **A monologue:** this is where you take the role of a character and talk to an audience about:
  - your life
  - the things that have happened to 'you' or may happen in the future
  - thoughts and feelings about 'your' experiences.
- **An interview:** this is where you take the role of a character and you are then interviewed by someone about:
  - the character
  - his or her life
  - the things that have happened to him or her, or may happen in the future
  - thoughts and feelings about his or her experiences.

Activity

6

a Choose a character from a text you have read or studied. It could be a novel, a play or a poem. Make a note of the different things you know about the character's background, personality, motivation, feelings and attitudes. You could record your notes in a character plan similar to the one you used earlier.

b Now think about the significant situations your character has been in. List these and make a note of how your character dealt with these situations.

c You are going to role play your chosen character and prepare a monologue to present to a group of students. Your purpose is to introduce yourself to them and tell them something about your life, the things that have happened to you and your thoughts and feelings about them. Before you do this you need to think carefully about:

- what you will say and the order in which you will say it
- how you will vary your body language
- how you will vary your tone of voice
- how you will get and keep your audience's attention.

Make notes on each of these bullet points and then rehearse your monologue. Aim to talk for about three minutes.

d You are now ready to present your monologue. Remember to stay in the role of your chosen character throughout your monologue.

Check your learning

1 With a partner, discuss and note the meanings of the following terms:
   a hot seating
   b motivation
   c improvised
   d scenario
   e monologue.

28

Making your speaking and listening skills count in the controlled assessment

Objectives

In this chapter you will:

learn about how speaking and listening fits into your GCSE course

explore the assessment objective for speaking and listening

look at the types of task you might undertake in your controlled assessment.

What is controlled assessment?

During the course, you will take part in many speaking and listening activities. At least three times during the course your teacher will **formally assess** you. These three assessments will each carry 15 marks. Together, the Speaking and listening controlled assessment mark counts for 20 per cent of your final GCSE grade.

Key terms

Formally assess: an official assessment that will count towards the final mark awarded.

Introducing the tasks

You will be assessed in three distinct areas. These are:

- presenting
- discussing and listening
- role playing.

The assessments your teacher will make are based on the Assessment Objectives. These are printed below and on the following page. The annotations will help you to understand what you need to do.

Show you can use language, tone of voice and body language to express your ideas

Be clear in what you say and make sure you achieve what you set out to do

Change what you say and how you say it to suit your audience and purpose

Organise and develop your ideas

Speak to communicate clearly and purposefully; structure and sustain talk, adapting it to different situations and audiences; use Standard English and a variety of techniques as appropriate.

Make sure you use standard English when appropriate

Use repetition, rhetorical questions, pausing for emphasis and other techniques to make your talk more effective

Listen to others and engage with their ideas and points of view

Listen and respond to speakers' ideas and perspectives and how they construct and express their meanings.

Consider both what they say and how they say it

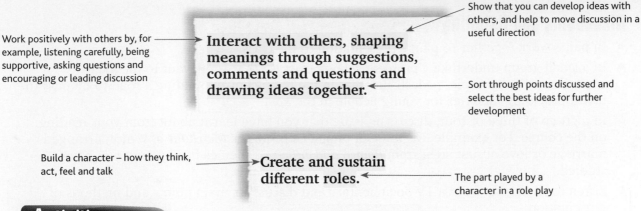

Work positively with others by, for example, listening carefully, being supportive, asking questions and encouraging or leading discussion

Interact with others, shaping meanings through suggestions, comments and questions and drawing ideas together.

Show that you can develop ideas with others, and help to move discussion in a useful direction

Sort through points discussed and select the best ideas for further development

Build a character – how they think, act, feel and talk

Create and sustain different roles.

The part played by a character in a role play

Activities

1 Think about the different skills highlighted in the Assessment Objectives. From these, list the three things you are best at.

2 The following are terms often used in connection with speaking and listening activities. Remind yourself of what they mean by matching the numbered points to the correct letters:

❶ Organisation

❷ Vocabulary

❸ Standard English

❹ Response to questions

❺ Participation

❻ Listening

ⓐ the form of English which will be recognised anywhere in the country

ⓑ the contribution you make through speaking, listening, making suggestions and asking questions

ⓒ taking on and maintaining the role of a character throughout an activity

ⓓ answering questions raised by others

ⓔ the choice of words you make

ⓕ the order into which you arrange what you want to say

The tasks

When you are being formally assessed your teacher will give you a specific task and you will usually have time to plan and prepare in advance. Here are examples of the types of tasks you might be asked to do.

Presenting

- Talk to the class about a topic of interest and then answer questions.
- Talk to the class as part of a paired presentation (you may be able to use ICT for this such as PowerPoint, visual media clips, etc.) and then answer questions on the presentation.
- Interview (or be interviewed by) an adult. The interview could focus on an aspect of work or a matter of local interest.
- Either listen to an extract of a speech on TV and then present the main points, or listen to a school assembly and present the main points and explain its methods of presentation.
- Give a speech to a wider audience (such as school assembly or another teaching group) either as an individual or as part of a team.

Discussing and listening

- In pairs, work together to plan a presentation to the class.
- In a small group undertake a problem-solving exercise that is relevant to the local community. For example, pedestrian areas in the town centre; building a road to by-pass the town; providing facilities for young people in the area.
- In a group of three or four, discuss an issue that you have learnt about from your reading on the course. For example, the issue of prejudice from *The Merchant of Venice*; arranged marriage or love at first sight from *Romeo and Juliet*; or themes from poetry you have studied.
- Listen to an extract from a TV documentary and discuss its main points and methods of presentation.

Role playing

- In role, perform an interview for TV or radio on a relevant issue, for example, an interview on 'Should students have to repay some of the cost of their university education?'
- In role, perform an interview between a detective and a suspect based upon a story from literature that you have studied previously.
- As a news presenter, perform a five-minute section for breakfast television called 'What the papers say today'.
- Perform an improvisation based on texts being studied. This could be performed individually or in groups.
- In small groups undertake a problem-solving exercise which is relevant to the local community, in which you each assume the role of an interested adult such as a parent, teacher, builder or councillor.

Activity

3 In pairs, think about each of the tasks listed above. Write down any of these that you have done as part of your GCSE studies. Add any speaking and listening tasks that you have done that are not listed above. Once your list is complete, highlight the task in which you did best and explain to your partner why you have highlighted it.

Thinking about assessment

Two students, Rashid and Imran, took part in an assessment task for *discussing and listening* where they were asked to discuss the benefits and drawbacks of building a new by-pass for the town where they live.

The summaries their teacher wrote about their performances are on page 187. Read them carefully.

Teacher's comments

Rashid

Vocabulary is quite straightforward and usually appropriate to task. Rashid was aware of the need for Standard English and generally used it where appropriate. He was clear in his responses to questions using some detail in the answers he gave. He made some useful contributions to the discussion and concentrated when listening to others.

Imran

In preparing for the task, Imran had organised what he wanted to say very clearly. His vocabulary and expression showed quite good variety and were appropriate to the task. His control over and use of Standard English were competent. His responses to questions or issues raised contained relevant and effective detail. Imran made a number of helpful contributions to the discussion. Although he never led the discussion, he did listen closely to others and respond appropriately to what they said.

Activity

4
a   Imran received a higher mark that Rashid for his part in the discussion. Can you list the reasons for this?

b   Imran did not get the best mark in his group. What do you think he needed to do in order to gain a higher mark?

c   Discuss your answers to **a** and **b** with a partner.

Top tip

The following points will help you prepare properly for an assessment. Think about:

- what to say and how to say it
- questions you might ask
- questions you might be asked
- what you might have to explain
- whether you need to use Standard English
- whether you need to create a character
- the need to practise and rehearse.

During your assessment make sure you:

- use Standard English if required
- speak clearly and not too quickly
- try to keep listeners interested
- listen carefully to what is being said and respond appropriately
- develop your own and others' ideas fully
- make significant contributions to discussions
- stay in role if appropriate
- take part effectively in creative activities.

Check your learning

With a partner, list 5–10 things you have learnt about the Speaking and listening controlled assessments.

Think about:

- Assessment Objectives
- types of tasks
- number of formal assessments
- number of marks awarded to formal assessments
- what your teacher will be giving marks for
- how you can prepare
- how your can do your best during your assessment.

Share your list with the rest of the class and amend your notes if you need to.

Section

D

Spoken language

Getting started

Sometimes the lines between speaking, listening, reading and writing are not clear. The different **modes** overlap. The study of spoken language is an investigative (questioning) approach to the way oral communication works. It gives you the opportunity to think about and find answers to the following questions:

Is this written English or spoken English?

Is he reading or listening?

Is she waiting for answers?

Why are these students talking in dialect?

Why is this student using Standard English?

How does he say his words?

What rules govern this writing?

This section of the book will help you to develop your understanding of spoken language. You will consider spoken language, both your own and that of other people, in the context of purpose and audience, and you will investigate the ways in which new technologies have blended (mixed) speaking and writing.

Aims of Spoken language section

The chapters in this section are designed to help you meet the Assessment Objectives that underpin your GCSE English Language course. These are written for teachers, but you might like to read them in full (they're explained in more detail on page 203).

- Understand variations in spoken language, explaining why language changes in relation to contexts.
- Evaluate the impact of spoken language choices in their own and others' use.

By the end of this section, you will have covered all of the skills outlined in the Assessment Objectives. By the end of your GCSE English Language course, you will have used these skills to help you gain the highest marks you can in your Spoken language study.

However, it doesn't stop there. This section will make you more aware of how other people speak and why they speak as they do. Using what you learn will not only help you listen more carefully to what people say and how they say it, it will also enable you to respond more appropriately and become a more effective user of language.

Key terms

Mode: usually used to mean whether a text is written or spoken.

29

Understanding the influences

Purpose and audience

As with written English, all forms of spoken English are determined by purpose and audience:

- **Purpose**: why you are speaking and what you hope to achieve through speech.
- **Audience**: the person or persons to whom you are speaking.

You would not speak in the same way when talking with a police officer as you would when talking with a friend. We all adapt our words, tone, body language and even our appearance to match the situation.

Activities

1 You are going to have an interview for a part-time job in a shop. Select items from the following list that would be important in having a successful interview.

> clear pronunciation   dialect   slouching position
>
> eye contact   appropriate clothing   Standard English
>
> sit up straight   arrive late   smart appearance
>
> casual clothes   friendly manner   bored expression
>
> punctuality   slang   yawn   smile
>
> knowledge about the shop

Check your selection with another student's and between you place the items in order of importance.

2 Write the first 5–10 words you would use if you were:

- attending the above interview
- meeting a friend in town
- asking a parent for a lift
- explaining to a teacher why your homework is late.

In an average day, we experience language in many different ways:

- We read it.
- We speak it.
- We hear it.
- We write it.

These experiences influence us and help to create our own individual way of talking. Your individual way of talking is called your **idiolect**.

Some of the things that most influence how a person speaks are:

- place of birth
- where the person now lives
- family
- friends and social groups.

Key terms

Idiolect: a person's individual way of talking.

Dialect: words used by people in one part of a country but not in the rest of it.

How place affects the way you speak

The places where we are born and where we live often have a major impact on the way we speak. Each area of the country has its own words and phrases that are not used elsewhere. They are not Standard English. A good example is the **dialect** words for the word 'child'. In different areas, a child is called a 'bairn', 'kid', 'nipper', 'tiddler', 'tyke', 'shaver', 'small fry' or 'nestling'.

With TV and other modern forms of communication, people are more aware of the words and phrases used in different parts of the country. Soaps such as *EastEnders* and *Coronation Street* both use dialogue filled with dialect words.

Activity

3

a How much dialect do you know? Look at the dialect words that have been put into sentences in the table (they are underlined). Copy and complete the table to show what you think they mean in Standard English. The first one has been done for you.

Dialect words	Meaning
I went up the <u>apples and pears</u>.	Stairs
Dad <u>put the kibosh</u> on us going.	
He's meeting <u>wer lass the neet</u>.	
I've got <u>sarnies</u> for <u>snap</u>.	
I was chatting on <u>the dog and bone</u>.	
I <u>divna kna</u>.	
Do <u>youse</u> know where the <u>khazi</u> is?	

b Discuss your answers with another student. Have you written the same things?

c With a partner, list 5–10 dialect words or phrases that are:

- used where you live
- used in other areas.

d In small groups, talk about the dialect you use in your own everyday speech. Decide whether each of you:

- always speaks in dialect
- often speaks in dialect
- sometimes speaks in dialect
- never speaks in dialect.

What different things affect why you may or may not speak in dialect?

As well as having different dialects, different regions can also have different **accents**. This means that the same sentence can contain exactly the same words, but it can sound completely different depending on the speaker's accent.

Key terms

Accent: the way a person pronounces (sounds) the words of the language. It is important to remember that whilst the sound changes, the words do not.

Activity

4

a In small groups, talk about and list the different accents you know and recognise. Where you can, try to describe the accent.

b Decide which of you has:
  - the strongest accent
  - the least strong accent.

c Individually, list one reason that would explain why you have a strong or not very strong accent.

How family affects the way you speak

For most people, the family is the first influence on the way a person speaks. Parents, grandparents, older brothers and sisters teach us words and how to put them together to communicate ideas. When we are little we learn new words at a faster rate than at any other time in our lives.

Some of us learn to speak another language before we learn English. Some of us learn English and another language at the same time. This can be a huge advantage in later life.

The people through whom we first learn to speak have a major impact on our idiolect. In Activity 5, you are going to investigate just a few of the ways in which your family has influenced your language.

Activity

5

a In small groups, list the different words you use for:
  - your grandparents, e.g. gran
  - mealtimes, e.g. lunch
  - rooms in your house, e.g. lounge
  - potatoes, e.g. spuds
  - sandwiches, e.g. sarnies
  - friends, e.g. pals.

Add any words that you know other students use to your list.

b Individually, make a separate list of the words you use for each of the above. Who taught you those words? Are there other words that are distinctive to you and your family? Add them to your list.

How social groups affect the way you speak

Key terms

Sociolect: a particular use of language specific to a social group.

As we grow older, the way we speak is influenced by the friends we make and the social groups to which we belong. Social groups may be small, such as friends at school, or large, such as Goths and Emos. The use of language specific to such a group is called a **sociolect**.

To join such a group you often need to adapt the way you speak. This is clearly seen in the following advice taken from a web site article on *How to Have a Skater Attitude* (Text A).

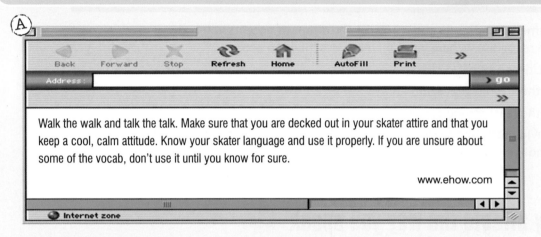

Walk the walk and talk the talk. Make sure that you are decked out in your skater attire and that you keep a cool, calm attitude. Know your skater language and use it properly. If you are unsure about some of the vocab, don't use it until you know for sure.

www.ehow.com

Many groups have their own way of talking and specific words that set them apart from other groups. For example, the following words would all be familiar to surfers:

| half pipes | bailing out | riding air | making a snap | walking the nose | wipe out |

If you want to pursue an interest, either for work or play, you need to know the vocabulary associated with it.

Activity

 6

a The words listed below would be part of the everyday vocabulary of:
- people who are familiar with ICT
- people who are interested in football.

They would not be regularly used in the same way by other people.

With a partner, sort the words into two groups under the headings: ICT/Football.

> DVD, offside, burn, defender, rip, foul, cookie, substitute, own goal, cyber crime, penalty, file sharing, league, search engine, goalkeeper, navigation bar, MP3, podcast, striker, hard drive, software, pitch, server, broadband, yellow card, Skype, touchline, tackle, handball, blog, draw, dotcom, dive, PC, corner kick, CD, referee, WiMAX.

b Identify and list the different social groups that you know about and/or belong to. These may be connected with sport, religion, music or particular subjects. They may be small or large.

c For each group, identify words or phrases that are commonly used by the individuals in that group. Share your findings with another pair.

How do you speak?

As mentioned earlier, a person's idiolect is influenced by many factors. Read the descriptions of some of the factors that have influenced Andrea's idiolect (Text B). The factors are annotated for you.

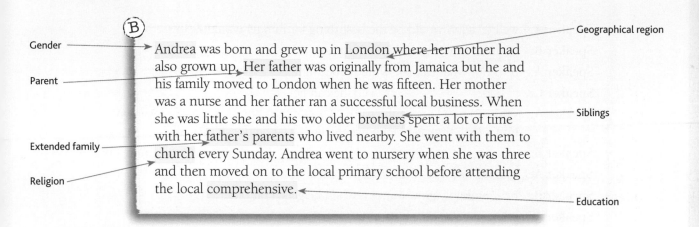

Gender

Parent

Extended family

Religion

(B) Andrea was born and grew up in London where her mother had also grown up. Her father was originally from Jamaica but he and his family moved to London when he was fifteen. Her mother was a nurse and her father ran a successful local business. When she was little she and his two older brothers spent a lot of time with her father's parents who lived nearby. She went with them to church every Sunday. Andrea went to nursery when she was three and then moved on to the local primary school before attending the local comprehensive.

Geographical region

Siblings

Education

Activity

7
a Using Text B as a model, write about yourself in the third person, i.e. 'John was …' Highlight and annotate the factors that have influenced your idiolect.

b For each factor that you have highlighted, give examples of how it has influenced the way you speak.

c Now think about any social factors that have influenced the way you speak, such as friends, groups, music, sport. For each one, give examples of how it has influenced the way you speak.

d With a partner, discuss what you have discovered about your idiolect.

Recording how you speak

When writing about your idiolect, or someone else's, you may be asked to produce a **transcript** of a conversation that illustrates some of the points you make.

The conventions for recording speech are different from those normally used in writing. This is partly because we don't always talk in sentences. We pause to gather our thoughts or to remember the word we want to use. We give emphasis to certain words by the way we say them. We also use sounds to fill gaps in the conversation such as 'mmm' or 'errm'. These are often referred to as **fillers**.

In the following **transcript** of a conversation (Text C) you can see some of the main conventions of recording speech. Use the key to help you read the transcript. Try to 'hear' it in your mind as you read.

Key terms

Transcript: a written record of a speech or conversation.

Filler: a sound, word or phrase used to fill a gap. For example, 'er', 'like', 'you know'.

(C)

Key:

(.) Micropause (less than a second)

(2) Longer pause (number of seconds indicated)

[ ] Simultaneous speech – where two or more people speak at the same time

Bold Emphatic stress

Speaker A: well (.) a job would be the best thing for him (.) wouldn't it?

Speaker B: mmmm well it would be if he gets it

Speaker A: b (.) but what can she write [about him]

Speaker C: [she can lie]

Speaker A: **yeah** (2) no (1) twist the truth (.) **you** write about him (.) she's known him a long time (1) he knows the family (.) he doesn't [steal]

Speaker B: [that we know of]

Speaker A: that we know of (.) he's very bright

Speaker B: he'll probably grow out of it when he gets a bit older

Speaker A: yeah

Check your learning

1 a With a partner, read aloud Text D, taken from a transcript of a conversation. Decide:

- where the pauses should be
- how long the pauses should be
- which words should be emphasised.

well like it was errm like there was no-one else there an it was all spooky like an I couldn't really see anything well there was a bit of light like but not enough to see

b Rewrite Text D using the approriate conventions.

c Now write the transcript of a conversation between you and your partner. Aim to write ten lines. Remember to use the conventions of transcript, including showing when you talk at the same time.

d Read through your transcript. Highlight and annotate any features of your speech that you think indicate your idiolect.

30

Multi-modal talk

Objectives

In this chapter you will:

learn about the impact of technology on spoken language

identify the features of texting

consider the relationship between instant messaging and spoken language

discuss the dangers and advantages of instant messaging.

In the first chapter of this section, you learnt about the factors that influence your own particular way of speaking (idiolect).

In this chapter, you are going to explore how technology has influenced the ways we communicate and has brought writing and speaking closer together.

The impact of technology

Thirty years ago a single computer would fill a room. Twenty years ago mobile phones were the size of bricks and texting didn't exist. Now many people use a desktop, or laptop, PC and a mobile phone. They text regularly and communicate on internet social networking web sites, such as Facebook, to set up **virtual communities**.

This rapid rise in widely-used technologies has led to dramatic changes in our language and the ways we use it. Thousands of 'new' words have been introduced.

> **Key terms**
>
> **Virtual communities:** groups of people who meet and connect on the Internet rather than in 'real' life.

- Some of these are combinations of words that already existed, such as 'website' and 'laptop'.
- Some are 'old' words that have been given a new meaning such as 'mouse' and 'text'.
- A few are completely new words such as 'iPod' and 'blog'.

Activity

1

a With a partner, read the following new words. They are combinations of words that already existed. Work out:

- which words are being combined
- the meanings of the words being combined
- the meaning of the new word.

> internet   web page   online   broadband   download
> podcast   network   ethernet   homepage

b The following words have been given a new meaning. For each one:

- work out the traditional meaning
- work out the new meaning.

> worm   mobile   virus   twitter   surf   server   spam

Texting

Texting, as a form of communication, has been around for a very short time. Your parents will not have used text, and probably wouldn't have heard of it, when they were your age. It is an area of communication in which young people are often expert.

Speaking and listening

1

In this activity, you are going to work in groups of three or four to find out what you know about texting. Follow these steps:

a Talk about when you text, how often you text and the reasons why you text. List three reasons to explain why texting is so popular.

b On paper, each member of the group should write a text they would send to a friend. These will provide the material for you to work out things about texting.

c Spread the 'texts' in front of you. Think about each of the features listed below. Can you find examples of them in your texts? Make a table with the feature in the first column and examples of it taken from your texts in the second column.

- Letters missed out of words (for example, tnght).
- Letters missed off ends of words (for example, goin).
- Single letters that sound like a word (for example, r – are).
- Numbers that sound like a word (for example, 2 – two, to, too).
- Words spelt the way they sound (for example, cud – could).
- Words spelt using a combination of letters and numbers (for example, l8r – later).
- Initial letters used (for example, lol – laugh out loud).
- Emoticons used to express feelings (for example, ☺).

d Are there any other features not listed above? Add them to your table.

Texting is developing and changing quickly. It is possible that in 50 years' time a student of your age will be trying to work out the meaning of the texts you send today.

Activity

2 Write a guide for a student in 50 years' time who is trying to understand the text messaging of today. Start with an explanation of why texting became so popular in the early years of the 21st century. Then explain the features of texting and give examples to help future students in their study.

Talking on the telephone

When you send a text message you say everything you want to and then wait for a reply. You may have to wait a while. It is not like a conversation. Telephones, unlike texting, have been around for some time. The first long-distance coast-to-coast telephone call was made in the USA in 1915. Since that time, the telephone gradually became a household feature. At first, people were uncertain how to use a telephone; they had never before spoken to a person without seeing them. Some put the mouthpiece to their ear. Others shouted down the telephone believing they had to make their voices carry a long distance.

Activity

3 Think about a conversation you would have with a friend who was with you. In what ways would the conversation be different if you were speaking on the telephone? What are the reasons for the differences?

We speak in different ways on the telephone. Depending on our purpose and audience, our conversations will be informal or formal. There are certain conventions, however, that are common to most telephone conversations. Read the transcripts of the following openings of two telephone conversations on page 198 (Texts A and B). The conventions that they have in common are annotated for you.

A

Informal

Karen: Hello? ❶

Sue: Hi Karen,❷ how you doing?

Karen: Errr …? ❸

Sue: It's Sue. ❹

Karen: Oh, hi Sue. Didn't recognise you for a minute. Yeah, I'm fine. How about you?

Sue: Oh not so bad. Just wanted to check with you about next week. ❺

❶ Start with a greeting.

❷ Caller checks identity of receiver.

❸ Receiver asks who is speaking.

❹ Caller reveals identity.

❺ Caller reveals reason for call.

B

Formal

Karen: Hello? ❶

Mrs Smith: Ah, good morning. Is that Mrs Jenkins, Guy's mother? ❷

Karen: Yes it is. Who's speaking please? ❸

Mrs Smith: This is Mrs Smith, Guy's form teacher. ❹

Karen: Oh, hello. There isn't a problem is there?

Mrs Smith: No, no problem. In fact, it's good news. He's just been selected for the county championships. ❺

Activity

 4

a Think about the telephone calls you make. Write the opening six lines of a typical call to someone who is not expecting you to call.

b Use the annotations shown in Texts A and B on your transcript where appropriate.

'Talking' online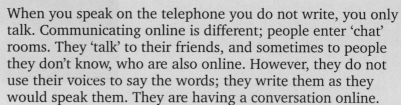

When you speak on the telephone you do not write, you only talk. Communicating online is different; people enter 'chat' rooms. They 'talk' to their friends, and sometimes to people they don't know, who are also online. However, they do not use their voices to say the words; they write them as they would speak them. They are having a conversation online.

Activity

 5

a Read Text C, a messaging transcript, and make a note of the features you would also find in texting.

b Here are some typical features of spoken and written texts. Which of these features can be used to describe the messaging text in Text C?

Written	**Spoken**
Received through the eyes	Received through the ears
Temporary	Permanent
Personal	Impersonal
Spontaneous	Planned

Activity

Would you describe the messaging text as:

- a spoken text
- a written text
- a mixture of both?

Explain the reasons for your choice.

c Look closely at the times when Beth, Natalie and daleo don't take turns to speak, and when the responses are not directly linked to what has come before. List reasons that would explain why this happens.

d Beth, Natalie and daleo often make clear how the words would be said either through spelling or punctuation. They want the others to 'hear' them. For example, daleo writes: 'hheeeyy'. Find and list other examples of this.

Beth says: Hey guys!!
Natalie says: hey!
Beth says: how are u?
Natalie says: im fine!
Beth says: u there d?
daleo says: hheeeyy
daleo says: im bacckkkk
Natalie says: wohoo!
Beth says: hey dale!
daleo says: what u both up to ☺
Beth says: just chillin, janes visiting!
daleo says: aww nice!!!
daleo says: say ello to jane to
Beth says: what are u up 2?
Natalie says: is that better?
Beth says: yey ☺
daleo says: yyeaa ☺
daleo says: hehe
daleo says: just chillin out tonight
daleo says: ☺
Natalie says: lol
daleo says: rite i have to go ☹ byyeeeeee
Beth says: hahahahaha mint
Beth says: aw ok bye bye ☺
+daleo has left the conversation

The dangers of talking too much

While talking online is done regularly by young people, it is still a new form of communication and there are concerns both about its use and its potential dangers.

Read these headlines:

Language Dumbed Down as Messaging Rises

STRANGER DANGER MOVES ONLINE

VIRTUAL LIVING PUSHES OUT REAL THING

FEARS FOR MISSING CHAT ROOM GIRL

BULLIES MOVE FROM CLASSROOM TO CHAT ROOM

CHAT ROOM ADDICTION ON INCREASE

Activity

6

a With a partner or in small groups, think and talk about the headlines above. What different concerns do they seem to be expressing about chat rooms?

b Basing your ideas on your own and friends' experiences, how valid do you think these concerns are? Give reasons for your answer.

c Which of these concerns do you consider to be the most and the least serious? Number them in order of priority, with the first being the most serious.

d Take your three most serious concerns. Agree and write some points of advice for people your age that would help to deal with these concerns.

What's next?

As you have seen, technology is changing the way we communicate. It is blurring the distinction between speaking and writing. The rapid development of texting and messaging makes it difficult to predict what will happen next. The only way to keep up with the changes is to keep doing it!

Check your learning

Many older people would like to use the new technologies to text and chat online. However, they are often frightened of them and lack the confidence to have a go. Write an advice sheet for older people that will give them the information they need to text and go online safely and help them to feel more confident. You can present your advice in any form you wish.

31

Making your spoken language study skills count in the controlled assessment

Objectives

In this chapter you will:

learn about how spoken language fits into your GCSE English Language course

explore the assessment objectives for spoken language

look at the types of tasks you might undertake in your controlled assessment.

What is controlled assessment?

If you are doing GCSE English Language, you will need to do a spoken language study as part of your course. This is a really exciting opportunity to explore language and see how it is used in modern society.

GCSE English Language

Controlled assessment title
Studying spoken language

Mark value
10% = 20 marks

Choice of task
One of:
- Social attitudes to spoken language
- Spoken genres
- Multi-modal talk.

Planning and preparation
You arc allowed to spend time discussing the texts and task, and you may make brief notes which can be taken into the controlled assessment.

Time for writing
Up to 3 hours

Expected length
800–1000 words

You will be allowed time to prepare for this task by gathering data in the form of transcripts or clips (audio/video) of language, which you have thought about and discussed in class with your teacher and other students. Suggestions for the type of information you will need to gather will be provided later in this chapter. You will be able to bring your transcripts with you when you complete the controlled assessment task, but you will not be able to bring notes, drafts or essay outlines.

Your preparation for the Spoken language controlled assessment will involve gathering information and evidence and then analysing that information using the following questions:
- How is this language used to communicate?
- Why is this language used to communicate?
- What is the purpose of this language?
- What are the key features of this language?
- What makes it different?
- How and why is it adapted for specific purposes?
- What is the public's attitude to this aspect of spoken language?

When you have gathered and analysed the information, you are in a position to write down your ideas about the key points above. It is important that when you are answering the above questions, you support your analysis with examples from your evidence.

Introducing the tasks

There are three choices of topic area for the spoken language study:

1 Social attitudes to spoken language.
2 Spoken genres.
3 Multi-modal talk.

There will be two task options for each topic you will complete one of these.

Assessment objectives

These are the criteria that your teacher and AQA, the exam board, will use to assess your work.

You will be expected to:

- Understand variations in spoken language, explaining why language changes in relation to contexts.

What does this mean?

This means that you need to be able to recognise that language changes in different situations and you need to be able to explain the reasons why it changes.

- Be able to evaluate the impact of spoken language choices in your own and others' use.

What does this mean?

This means that you need to analyse, make judgements on (give an opinion) and present your findings on using language in different situations.

Preparing for the controlled assessment

Through the spoken language study you will learn more about how language works. The emphasis of the study is on what is happening in the world of language, now!

Choosing a task

Areas you could study might include:

- a younger brother or sister's speech development
- language as used in a soap opera
- language as used in a TV news programme
- a study of your own idiolect
- different modes of language used in different genres of television programmes
- a study of jargon, looking at work-specific language.

Whichever task you choose, make sure that you have enough information to work with and that you keep the assessment criteria firmly in mind. In your task, you should:

- show that you know why people speak in different ways at different times and in different places
- comment on the effects of the language that people choose to use.

Analysing your information

To do well you need to think carefully about the words people use and how they use them when working with data. You will need to note different things. For example:

- word use: how and why different words are used
- frequency of words
- jargon words
- word deviations in text or MSN speak.

Sample tasks and answers

In your written assessment, you need to be able to:

- explain, analyse and evaluate what you have been studying
- show your understanding of the data.

To do well you will need to do more than simply describe your research and explain your data.

You must give your teacher evidence that you can explain and evaluate what you have studied. The more *selective* you are about this the better – don't simply quote chunks of text or data the best essays select certain words to *illustrate* their points and embed them in sentences.

When planning your response, you should bear the following basic structure in mind:

- **Introduction**: a brief outline of the background.
- **Key points**: these should be linked and explored.
- **Conclusion**: a few key sentences that bring together the main points you have made.

The introduction is deliberately brief and means that you have a structure for all three responses. However, you are not being led to think in a particular way; you can write as you wish. The important thing is to introduce and conclude your work and make sure that the points you make are clear and linked. Your conclusion will complete your essay by simply tying together the points that you have made. It is a good way of making a final point about your thoughts.

Social attitudes to spoken language

We all tend to speak differently in different situations. There are words that you use when you are with your friends that you might not use with parents or grandparents.

You will be asked to choose a topic and complete only one task from this area. The key words for this topic will be 'reflect' or 'investigate'.

- **Reflect** means that you will need to think about why certain language is used in certain situations and share this in your written work.
- **Investigate** means that you will need to explore and examine the spoken language area that you choose and share this in your written work.

Here is a sample task from this topic area. Remember, your teacher will be looking for your understanding of the work. They will also be looking for your ability to analyse, explore and explain what you have discovered.

> 1 Record a conversation with someone from an older generation about their memories of summer holidays. Investigate the way that they express their views.

Read Text A, **part of** a student's response to this task in the topic area of Social attitudes to language change, and the teacher's comment that follows.

Introduction

Uncle Trevor has worked hard for all of his life and has recently bought a house in France. He is 75 years old and I interviewed him to find out how he used to holiday when he was a child. I was very interested in the language that he used to describe his holidays, as Uncle Trevor is a Cockney and I remember being very interested in the way he spoke when I was little.

Paragraph suggestion

He mentioned money a few times when he spoke. He talked about 'savings'. This interested me because it seemed to be very natural to him. You only seem to hear this sort of thing in the news now, most people talk about spending. He also said that the first holiday they had was to Butlins at Clacton when it opened in 1938. He seemed very excited when talking about this and kept mentioning that his old Dad had had to save up a 'beehive' for the family to go for a week. This put a funny picture in my head and I thought how many pictures words can make. He went on to explain that a 'beehive' was a fiver – Cockney rhyming slang for 'five'. There were lots of comments about 'bees' and I thought that the words must have something to do with being busy and working hard. He also talked a lot about 'saving the coppers' and his 'Post Office savings book'. All of this really interested me because his language was really colourful and showed very clearly how much people were focused on saving when he was a boy.

Conclusion

Uncle Trevor focused on main areas, which made his speech interesting and particular to his age and the time that he was talking about. Many of the words were very colourful and some are rarely heard now, even though they were very common when he was younger. This shows how spoken language changes very quickly, especially now when there are so many more things like TV and the Internet to interest people. It was particularly interesting that his language really focused on the points that were interesting to him and this is when he became very lively and started using a more imaginative vocabulary. This shows how powerful our language actually is.

Teacher's comment

There are many positive points here: noticing the focus on certain topics of words; commenting on changes over time; commenting on the effects of the chosen language and being able to place the memories in the context of when Uncle Trevor was young.

This piece shows understanding of the use of language and the context.

It is beginning to explore. More could be made of this by looking in detail at the origins of some of the words and how they have changed over time in spoken language, for example.

This could be built on by taking time to make a deeper analysis. A focus point for this could be the differences between the spoken and written language, which is already identified by the candidate.

More depth of analysis would make it easier for the candidate to explain the main points of the question.

Activity

1 Think about what you are being shown in the sample answer above (Text A). With a partner, rewrite the answer to include some of the improvements that the teacher has suggested.

Spoken genres

This topic area has many similarities with Social attitudes to spoken language. For example, it asks you to explore how language works in different situations and for different reasons.

You will be asked to choose a topic and complete only one task from this area. The key words for this topic will be 'how' is something 'represented', or 'investigate'.

- **How** encourages you to explore what the writers are doing to make something real to an audience. This is why it is linked with 'represent', which means that the language stands for something – it might represent the people of suburban Manchester (*Coronation Street*). What you are being asked to show your teacher is 'how' this is done.

- **Investigate** means that you will need to explore and examine the topic area that you choose and share this in your written work.

Here is a sample task from this topic area. Remember, your teacher will be looking for your understanding of the work. They will also be looking for your ability to analyse, explore and explain what you have discovered.

> 2 Look at a speech by George Graham Vest and comment on how it communicates with the audience.

Read Text B, part of a student's response to this task in the topic area of Spoken genres, and the teacher's comment that follows.

(B)
Introduction
This is an interesting and short speech that is old but it is still easy to understand the thoughts behind it in the modern day. It has a simple structure, which makes it easy to follow, but it says interesting things in a clever way.

Paragraph suggestion
The writing moves from negative thoughts about people to positive thoughts about the loyalty of a dog. He starts off by writing about men 'turn[ing] against him', being his 'enemy', 'ungrateful', and 'traitors'. All of these words make the listener or reader feel cold and add to the contrast when he goes on to talk about the dog. He writes that the dog 'stands by him', 'remains', is 'constant' and 'faithful'. Both groups of words are repeated to add to their force and have a better effect on the audience. It is easier, then, to see the contrast between the two parts of the speech.

Conclusion
Words are used to make the audience think and make them focus on the point that the speaker is making. They are carefully chosen and structured in such a way that they have a bigger effect on the audience and really make people think.

Teacher's comment

This piece of work demonstrates some awareness of how language can be used to persuade. It shows an awareness of the significant features found in this area of spoken language. There is also an awareness of the effects of time on language change.

Good understanding is shown, but much more could be made of the points that are identified. At the moment they are simply two lists of words which show that the candidate is aware of the contrast between them. By taking individual words and linking them to connotations (ideas linked to a word in context), much more could be made of this and the candidate could begin to move into the area of a clear and consistent explanation. At present, this does too much of spotting words and not enough of actually exploring.

Activity

2   Note down the words that are quoted from the speech in Text B. For example, 'enemy' and 'faithful'. These are positive and negative words. Write a couple of short paragraphs to explain why these words are so powerful.

Multi-modal talk

This is an area in which many of you may well be particularly interested. This allows you to explore and explain things like instant messaging, text speak, chat rooms (and the language used in them) and many other areas that are linked into this area of spoken/written communication. It is an area that is fast moving and literally evolving as it is used.

You will be asked to choose a topic and complete only one task from this area. The key words for this topic will be 'how', relating to the 'practicalities' of the actual 'communication'.

- **How** encourages you to explore exactly what is done in this language to allow people to chat with one another.
- **Practicalities** means the actual facts about how people communicate when it is not face to face.
- **Communication** means to explain what we do when we share information with each other.

Here is a sample task from this topic area. Remember, your teacher will be looking for your understanding of the work. They will also be looking for your ability to analyse, explore and explain what you have discovered.

> 3   What are the differences between messaging/texting and normal written communication? How do these differences make messaging/texting closer to spoken rather than written language?

Read Text C, part of a student's response to a task in the topic area of Multi-modal talk, and the teacher's comment that follows.

(C)

Introduction

Differences in why messaging or texting are used means that there are differences in words used and how those words are spelt. There is also no need for punctuation in messaging or texting. Messaging or texting is normally used between friends and not for other reasons. This means that there is more room for a relaxed style.

Paragraph suggestion

One of the differences between messaging or texting and normal written language is that it can be quite short and almost rude.

SH (stuff happens), PONA (person of no account) and NMP (not my problem) are three examples of the rudeness and shortness which is part of this. They are short and snappy, something which you might find in a conversation moving quickly through different subjects as young people chat. The sharpness is also something that would be unusual in a normal conversation. The removal of rules and structure makes this rudeness seem worse. This is probably one of the many reasons why some adults are not happy with messaging and texting.

Conclusion

Messaging and texting are communications that are somewhere between writing and speech. They have points that are the same as speech, including speed; but can be confusing and not as clear as speech.

Teacher's comment

This piece of work shows some awareness of how language varies in times or places. It also shows an awareness of language that is specific to a group (sociolect).

The candidate highlights a number of interesting points but never really takes them to any depth, so there is no evidence of a clear and consistent explanation. This could be achieved by taking the individual points that are made and beginning to explore them in more depth rather than simply moving on to another point. For example, the part about the abbreviated (shortened) speech could be used to explore the effects of this style of language in much more detail. Comment can be made on the differences between this and a standard use of language and how this makes people feel. This would then move the essay on clearly and consistently.

Check your learning

In this chapter you have:

- learned about how spoken language fits into your GCSE English Language course
- learned about the assessment objectives and how to prepare for the controlled assessment
- looked at sample tasks, student answers and teacher comments.

Punctuation makes it easier for the reader to follow your writing. This chapter shows you how to punctuate your writing using a range of punctuation marks. The activities give you the opportunity to practise what you have learnt.

Punctuation

Capital letters

Capital letters are used:

- to mark the start of a sentence

> He knocked on the door. An old woman opened it slowly.

- for the personal pronoun 'I'

> If I miss the bus, I'll text you.

- for the first letter of proper nouns (people's names, place names, names of days and months)

> She knew that Karen had met Sophie in Newcastle on Thursday.

- for the first letter of titles of people and organisations

> They asked Doctor Owen to attend Oxfam's next meeting.

- at the beginning of a new piece of direct speech

> Sadly, he replied, 'The house was empty when we arrived.'

- for the main words in titles of books, plays, games, films, etc.

> The boy thought *The Lord of the Rings* was the best film he'd seen.

Full stops

The main use of a full stop is to mark the end of a sentence:

> The street was dark and silent.
> No one spoke a word.

Question marks and exclamation marks

These can both be used at the end of sentences.
- The question mark is used to mark the end of a question.
- The exclamation mark is used to show expression.

> How old are you?

> Get out now!

Activity

1

a The following paragraph has been written without capital letters and the ends of sentences have not been marked. Rewrite it punctuating it correctly.

> how many times must we hear the same old argument teenagers always say their friends are allowed to do the things we won't allow them to is this really true yesterday, my son chris asked if he could go to a party in newquay and stay overnight he said that all his friends were going however, when i rang Maggie, his best friend's mother, she said her son had said exactly the same thing enough is definitely enough it's time for parents to fight back

b Read your punctuated version aloud. It should make clear sense. If it does not, you need to rethink where you have placed your punctuation marks.

Commas

Commas help the reader to follow a sentence. We use commas to:

- separate items on a list. When you write lists in a sentence you need to separate the items with commas. The final comma, before the 'and', is usually left out. For example:

> The cupboard was crammed full of sports shoes, footballs, cycling helmets, golf clubs and even some scuba diving equipment.

- mark off extra information. When you give extra information about something or somebody, you use commas to separate it from the main sentence. For example:

> Jane Simons, 28, claimed she had bought the gold watch as a gift for her mother. Mrs Simons, mother of two, was unable to show a receipt and Police Constable Watson, the arresting officer, asked her to accompany him to the station.

- separate different parts of a sentence. Commas help the reader to make sense of what you have written. They mark a pause, the same way as you would pause when speaking. For example:

> Although the sun was shining, she still packed her umbrella.

Activity

2

The commas have been left out of the following extract from a computer manual. Read the paragraph aloud and decide where the commas need to be placed to make clear sense of the writing. Rewrite the paragraph, placing the commas correctly.

> Your computer can catch a virus from disks a local network or the Internet. Just as a cold virus attaches itself to a human host a computer virus attaches itself to a program. And just like a cold it is contagious. Like viruses worms replicate themselves. However instead of spreading from file to file they spread from computer to computer infecting an entire system.

© Norton antivirus booklet

Apostrophes

The apostrophe is used to show:

- where one or more letters have been missed out. Instead of saying 'I am' we often use the shortened form of 'I'm'. The apostrophe is used in writing to show that a letter or letters have been missed out. For example:

we are → we're	is not → isn't
they have → they've	cannot → can't

The apostrophe is placed in the exact spot where the missing letter or letters would have appeared.

- that something belongs to someone or something (possession). We rarely say 'the house of my friend'. We would be more likely to say 'my friend's house'. In this case, the apostrophe is used to show that the house belongs to the friend. The *friend* is the possessor. Where you place the apostrophe depends on whether the possessor is singular or plural.

Top tip

There are a few commonly used words that don't follow the normal rule:

Will not → won't

Shall not → shan't

- Singular:
  When the possessor is singular, as in the case of 'Paul', the apostrophe is placed after the word and 's' is added. For example:

  the friend of Paul → Paul's friend

- Plural, ending in 's':
  When the possessor is plural and already ends in 's', we just add an apostrophe. For example:

  the school of the girls → the girls' school

- Plural, not ending in 's':
  When the possessor is plural but does not end in 's', we add an apostrophe and 's'. For example:

  the children of the men → the men's children

Activity

The following passage should contain three apostrophes to show omission and six apostrophes to show possession. Rewrite the passage putting the apostrophes in the correct places.

> Johns mother had told him that he wasnt allowed to go to Peters house that day. If he did, the postman wouldnt be able to deliver the parcel she was expecting. However, while she was at work, hed borrowed his brothers bike and gone straight there. There was no one in, though the younger childrens toys were still out on the lawn. Peters window was open and John climbed in through it, intending to wait for him. Unfortunately for John, he was spotted by the neighbours dog and then by the neighbour.

Inverted commas

Inverted commas are also sometimes referred to as speech marks or quotation marks. Most punctuation marks sit on the line of the page. Inverted commas hang in the air. They can be single, or double.

There are two main times when inverted commas are used:

1   When a writer uses a speaker's actual words.

2   When a writer is quoting from another text.

'single inverted commas'

"double inverted commas"

Study the use of inverted commas in the following very short story *What's Wunce?* Check that the rules written below it are followed correctly in the story.

What's Wunce?

'Once,' began the teacher.
'What's wunce?' asked the little girl.
'Once,' repeated the teacher.
'Can you eat it?'
'Listen!' said the teacher. 'Once upon …'
'What's a pon?' asked the little girl.
'Upon,' repeated the teacher.
'Can you play with it?'
'Listen!' said the teacher. 'Once upon … a time.'
'A-time,' said the little girl. 'B-time. C-time. Words are so strange.'

Kevin Crossley-Holland, *Book of Very Short Stories*, Oxford University Press

The rules:

● Each piece of speech begins and ends with inverted commas.

● When there is a new speaker, the writer starts a new line.

● Every new piece of speech starts with a capital letter.

● Every piece of speech ends with a punctuation mark.

4

a In Text B, a student is writing about Philip Larkin's poem 'Born Yesterday' in the AQA Anthology. Read a copy of the poem and study the student's writing and the annotations that surround it.

Ⓑ

> Larkin wrote this poem for a new-born girl who he refers to as a 'tightly-folded bud'. This image reminds us that her life has yet to unfold. He wants to wish something for her but wants to avoid the 'usual stuff' that 'they will all wish you'. His wish is an unusual one. He wishes that she should be 'ordinary'. In doing so he believes he is wishing for:
>
> 'Nothing uncustomary
>
> To pull you off your balance'.

Quotation marks are placed before and after the words taken from the poem

More than one quotation can be used in the same sentence

A quotation can be used to give emphasis to a particular word or phrase

A colon can be used to introduce a longer quotation

b Read the next few lines of the same student's writing. The quotations have been underlined. Copy the lines, adding inverted commas and a colon where needed.

> It is as though Larkin believes that <u>being beautiful</u> can be <u>unworkable</u>. In contrast being <u>not ugly, not good-looking</u> can bring greater happiness, perhaps because you put more effort into being happy. It is for this reason that he wishes she should
>
> <u>Have, like other women,</u>
>
> <u>An average of talents.</u>

Spelling

This chapter gives you some basic rules and some strategies to use to help you spell correctly. The activities give you the opportunity to practise what you have learnt.

Syllables

A syllable is a unit of sound. A word might contain:

- one syllable
- many syllables

❶ mud

❶ ❷ ❸ ❹ en/ter/tain/ment

❶ ❷ ❸ ❹ po/lit/i/cal

Breaking a word into syllables and sounding each syllable aloud will help you spell the word correctly. For example, saying the word diff/i/cult aloud reminds you of the letter *i* in the middle.

Activity

5

a Copy the following words. Break them into syllables, using a forward slash (/) and numbers as shown above. Say them aloud to make sure you have identified the syllables correctly.

absolutely	possible	chocolate
prejudice	interesting	different

b Ask a partner to test you on spelling the six words.

Suffixes

A suffix is a letter or group of letters added to the end of a root word, which changes the meaning of the word. Some frequently-used suffixes are:

-ly -able -ed -ful -ing -ment -ness -ity

In most cases, you simply add the suffix to the root word, for example:

spend → spending   care → careful   appoint → appointment

Make a note

There are some exceptions you need to learn:

If the word ends in a *c*, add *k* when you add a suffix beginning with *e*, *i* or *y*

For example: picnic → picnicked

When adding the suffix *-ful* or *-ly* to words that end in a consonant followed by *y*, change the *y* to *i*.
For example: plenty → plentiful   happy → happily

When a suffix begins with a vowel or a *y* and the root word ends in *e*, drop the *e*.
For example: write → writing   ease → easy   fame → famous

However, when the root word ends in *ee*, *oe* or *ye*, you keep the final *e*.
For example: agree → agreeable   canoe → canoeing

When you add the suffix *able* to a root word that ends in *ce* or *ge* you keep the final *e*.
For example: notice → noticeable   change → changeable

Consonants are sometimes doubled when you add *-ar*, *-er*, *-ed* or *-ing* to a word that has one syllable and ends with a short vowel and any consonant except *y* or *x*.
For example: run → running, hit – hitting, beg → beggar, rob → robber

If the word ends in *y* or *x* do not double the consonant.
For example: play → playing   tax → taxed

Activity

6

a Look again at the list of commonly used suffixes. What new words can you make from the following by adding one or more suffixes to them?

> wonder   reason   dread   favour   astonish

b Check you have learnt the exceptions by completing the following:

- Add the suffix *-ing* to the following words:

  panic   traffic   make   date   guarantee   slice   sit   tap   put

- Add the suffix *-ful* to the following words:

  bounty   play   beauty

- Add the suffix *-able* to the following words:

  challenge   balance   debate   pronounce

- Add the suffix *-ed* to the following words:

  bar   sob   fax   tan   net

Prefixes

A prefix is a group of letters that can be added to the beginning of a word to change its meaning.

> spell misspell   appear disappear   happy unhappy

Activity

7

Some of the most common prefixes are listed in the first column of the table below. Match these to the base words in the second column to make new words. Some base words work with more than one prefix, for example *dis*appear, *re*appear. The base words are in groups of ten. Work through one group before moving on to the next. See how many new words you can form in five minutes.

Prefix	Base word				
re mis in	1	behave like	place organise	trust obedient	order responsible	honest kind
sub im anti	2	social healthy	clockwise fortunate	aware form	able insure	conscious produce
ir dis un	3	effective polite	equality possible	secure rational	proper regular	material standard

214

Combining prefixes and suffixes

Knowing how to use and spell prefixes and suffixes correctly gives you access to a wide range of words. For example:

success	honest	satisfy
successful	honesty	satisfied
successfully	honestly	satisfying
unsuccessful	dishonest	satisfiable
unsuccessfully	dishonesty	satisfaction
	dishonestly	satisfactory
		satisfyingly
		unsatisfied
		dissatisfy
		unsatisfactory

Activity

8

Using the table to help you, make as many words as you can using the root words, a prefix and one or more suffixes.

Prefix	Root word	Suffix
re	agree	able
mis	fair	ment
in	reverse	ly
sub	sense	ed
im	perfect	ful
anti	skill	ing
ir		ion
dis		ible
un		less

Plurals

Plural means more than one. For most plural forms, you simply add 's' to the singular forms. For example:

book → books   computer → computers

Make a note

There are some exceptions you need to learn:

■ When the singular form ends in -*s*, -*x*, -*ch* or -*sh*, add -*es*.
For example: bus → buses   tax → taxes   church → churches   flash → flashes

■ If a word ends in -*y* and has a **consonant** before the last letter, change the *y* to an *i* and add *es*.
For example: party → parties   fly → flies

■ If a word ends in -*o* you usually just add *s*. However, there are a few commonly used words that need *es* to make them plural:
  ■ tomato → tomatoes
  ■ potato → potatoes
  ■ hero → heroes

■ If a word ends in -*f* or -*fe* you usually change the -*f* or -*fe* to -*ves*.
For example: wolf → wolves   knife → knives.

But there are a few exceptions:
  ■ roof → roofs
  ■ chief → chiefs
  ■ reef → reefs

There are some irregular plurals, many of which you will already know:

child → children	man → men	formula → formulae
sheep → sheep	mouse → mice	crisis → crises
tooth → teeth	person → people	stimulus → stimuli

Activity

9

a Using the above rules, write the plurals of the following words:

> branch   holiday   Christmas   beach   radius
> lady   atlas   inch   woman   blush   comedy
> cactus   takeaway   hoax   witch   berry
> bonus   plus   essay   gas   arch

b Now write the plurals of the following words:

> dash   crunch   disc   trolley   woman   ox
> proof   baby   life   axis   domino   fax   screen
> half   spy   lunch   belief   desk   wife

Glossary

Accent: the way a person pronounces (sounds) the words of the language. It is important to remember that whilst the sound changes, the words do not.

Adjective: describing words that tell you more about a noun – for example, the *tired* boy ran slowly.

Adverb: words that give details about how a verb is being done – for example, the boy ran *slowly*.

Atmosphere: used to describe the feelings or emotions suggested by a text – for example threatening, romantic, tense, etc.

Audience: an author writes with a particular person or group of people in mind: this is the intended audience.

Autobiography: the story of a person's life written by him or herself.

Bold print: used to make certain words stand out.

Bullet point: used to list details.

Cackle: Harsh high-pitched sound or laugh (often suggesting pleasure at the misfortune of another).

Clause: a group of words that expresses an event or a situation. A sentence is made up of one or more clauses. A main clause is complete on its own and can form a complete sentence.

Content: what the text is about – the subject of the text.

Criteria: things on which we base our judgements.

Culture: a set of shared beliefs and values that define a group of people and shape their behaviour and ways of thinking.

Device: a writing method used for a particular purpose.

Dialect: words used by people in one part of a country but not in the rest of the country.

Dialogue: words that are spoken by characters.

Drama: a play written to be acted on a stage or made into a TV or film production.

Effect: what the audience feels or does as a result of seeing the text.

Evaluate: to make a judgement on something based on evidence.

Fact: something that can be proved to be true.

Feature: something about a text that you can comment on – for example, features of a leaflet might be the layout, the language used or the colours used.

Filler: a sound, word or phrase used to fill a gap. For example, 'er', 'like', 'you know'.

First-person narrative: writing from the single point of view of a narrator using 'I', 'me', 'my', 'we' and 'our'. This gives the reader only one opinion of what is happening and lets them know the thoughts and feelings of the narrator.

Form: refers to the way writing is structured and organised on the page.

Formal language: where the speaker takes great care to match language choice and grammar to the context, audience and purpose of the talk. It does not (normally) include slang or abbreviations.

Formally assessed: an official assessment that will count towards the final mark awarded.

Functional skill: a skill that enables people to operate effectively in the workplace and in social situations.

Genre: the style of something. In writing, this could be crime, horror, etc.

Gesture: a movement of the hands, head or body to express or emphasise an idea or emotion.

Hyperactivity: used to describe someone who is constantly active and excitable.

Idiolect: a person's own personal language, the words they choose and any other features that mark out their speech.

Impact: the reaction that an audience has to a feature or features of a text.

Improvised: where everything that is to happen or be spoken is not written down in advance.

Mode: usually used to mean whether a text is written or spoken.

Mood: used to describe the feelings or emotions suggested by a text – for example threatening, romantic, tense, etc.

Motivation: the reasons people have for speaking and behaving in the ways they do.

Noun: a word that denotes somebody or something. For example, the *boy* ran.

Novel: a long piece of writing in prose; usually a fiction story.

Obese: very overweight.

Opinion: a person's view about something – for example, Italy is the best place to visit on holiday or science-fiction films are better than romantic comedies.

Plot: what the story is about, the storyline.

Prose: the usual way that writing or speech is recorded; not poetry or drama.

Punctuation: the marks and letters used to show how text should be read. Different marks mean different things.

Purpose: the reason why the text has been written – for example to inform or entertain.

Realistic: similar to events or speech in real life.

Scanning: reading a text quickly to pick out specific details.

Scenario: an outline of a situation, setting and the characters involved.

Scripted: where everything that is to happen or be spoken is written down in advance.

Sequence: the order that something is done or events happen; the way actions are carried out in a specific way.

Setting: place or places where the story happens.

Short story: a shorter piece of writing in prose; often with a 'twist' at the end.

Simple sentence: at its most simple, contains one subject and one verb.

Skimming: reading a text quickly to get an idea of what it is about.

Slang: words or phrases that are used when speaking or writing informally, often linked with certain regions or used by certain groups of people.

Sociolect: a particular use of language specific to a social group.

Standard English: the variety of English usually used by public figures (such as the Queen and newsreaders). It is not limited to a particular region and can be spoken with any accent.

Statistics: a piece of information shown as a number.

Subheadings: used to divide text into sections.

Subject: a topic which is being described, discussed or written about.

Subjugated: Brought under control.

Subordinate clause: this is connected to the main clause and cannot exist on its own.

Synonym: a word or phrase that means the same, or almost the same, as another word.

Text style: the way the words look – for example, choice of font, size and shape.

Tone: a writer's attitude towards the subject and/or audience – for example, serious, humorous, angry or sad.

Topic sentence: a sentence used at the start of a paragraph that shows what the paragraph will be about.

Transcript: a written record of a speech or converstaion.

Type two diabetes: an inability to properly regulate blood sugar levels.

Uncouth: Behaving in an ill-mannered, unrefined way (being awkward or clumsy).

Verb: a word that shows an action or state. For example, jump, walk, think, am.

Verb tense: the way a verb shows the different times at which events take place. For example, 'he was here' is the past tense because it is something that has already happened.

Virtual communities: groups of people who meet and connect on the Internet rather than in 'real' life.

Vocabulary: words used in a text, which are chosen to have an impact on the reader.